THE GENTLEMAN SAVAGE

THE GENTLEMAN SAVAGE

The Life of Mansfield Parkyns 1823–1894

Sir Duncan Cumming

CENTURY

London Melbourne Auckland Johannesburg

Copyright © Ann Schlee 1987

First published in 1987 by Century Hutchinson Ltd
62–65 Chandos Place, Covent Garden, London WC2N 4NW

Century Hutchinson Australia Pty Ltd
PO Box 496, 16–22 Church Street, Hawthorn, Victoria 3122,
Australia

Century Hutchinson New Zealand Ltd
PO Box 40-086, Glenfield, Auckland 10, New Zealand

Century Hutchinson South Africa (Pty) Ltd
PO Box 337, Bergvlei 2012, South Africa

Typeset by Inforum Ltd, Portsmouth
Printed and bound in Great Britain by
Anchor Brendon Ltd, Tiptree, Essex

British Library Cataloguing in Publication Data
Cumming, Sir Duncan
The gentleman savage : the life of
Mansfield Parkyns 1823-1894.
1. Parkyns, Mansfield   2. Travellers —
Great Britain — Biography
I. Title
910.4'092'4   G246.P3/

ISBN 0-7126-1734-5

Contents

Acknowledgements

The Gentleman Savage is compiled from a larger work about four English travellers in Abyssinia on which my father was working at the time of his death in 1979. So many people had helped him with his researches over a lifetime of interest in this subject that he had planned to devote an appendix to acknowledgements. Sadly he did not achieve this. I can only mention those names known to me and am all too aware that there are many others he would have wished to add. I can only trust that those whose names are omitted will understand this and accept the gratitude I know he felt.

He was particularly indebted to Mansfield Parkyns' descendants for their interest and encouragement. Mrs Armstrong, Mrs Lodge and the late Mrs Tyser generously allowed him access to the family portraits and to Mansfield Parkyns' water colours, wood-carvings and manuscript journal. Ato Ambaye Gezeheyn John gave him details of the subsequent history or Parkyns' Ethiopian descendant.

Mrs Dorothy Middleton, Dr Richard Pankhurst and Professor Charles Beckingham at various times read the typescript and were generous with their expert knowledge of travel and Ethiopian history. He was in correspondence with and often helped by Sir Edward Ullendorff and Dr Richard Hill. He had assistance over family and county history from Nottingham County Library and the Thoroton Society, and relied greatly on the resources of the Royal Geographical Society where he mentioned particularly the help of Mrs Christine Kelly.

Mrs Emma Baity, Leila Sandford, Jennifer Raison and Catherine Schlee at various times helped with their typing, and their interest.

I should like to add my personal thanks to Mrs Lodge, Dr Pankhurst, Mrs Middleton, Dr Hemming of the Royal Geographical Society, Sir Edward Peek and Dr Juel-Jensen for their kindness and help in bringing this book to publication and to Victoria Huxley for her sympathetic editing.

Ann Schlee, London 1987

Introduction

As the cool early months of 1843 turned into hot summer, Dr Walne, the British vice-consul in Cairo, observed with a hint of complaint that Egypt had experienced an influx of tourists. This was an exaggeration, but one may sympathize with Dr Walne because most of the British tourists regarded themselves as persons of sufficient consequence to deserve his personal attention. In fact, there had been twenty-two sailing craft on the Nile during the season, carrying about fifty British tourists to view the antiquities in Upper Egypt; more than usual, it is true, as a consequence of the improved steamship services across the Mediterranean. Waterborne expeditions of this kind had the reputation of providing exotic experiences without imposing too much physical discomfort for, as one of the visitors observed, 'a boat on the Nile combines the gentility of the yacht with the tranquility of the barge'. According to their tastes, the visitors of 1843 puzzled over the intricacies of Egyptology, savoured the fading romanticism of Byron's Orient, or indulged themselves more prosaically. They took the opportunity to relax conventional standards: grew beards, wore turbans and smoked long Turkish pipes, happy to behave whimsically so far from home.

What brought them to Egypt? Two simple reasons were that they wanted to travel and that they could afford the fare. No doubt some of them hoped to extend their intellectual range. A few were purposeful. Eliot Warburton, for example, was collecting material for a book, *The Crescent and the Cross*, that was widely read when it was published the following year. Lady Louisa Tenison was searching unsuccessfully for literary inspiration in wisps of tobacco smoke. Richard Dadd had come to paint. Richard Monckton Milnes was smarting from a reverse to his promising political career and hoping to redeem the errors of his judgement of the Eastern Question by parading at Westminster first hand acquaintance with the people of the East, who were usually overlooked by those who tried to find an answer to the 'question' in the West. The tourists were not a distinguished group, but at least they had the initiative, as well as the means, to make a journey that was still unusual.

Might it not be expected, therefore, that some of them would now be remembered? Students of Victorian letters are familiar with the name, if not the works, of Richard Monckton Milnes. Richard Dadd, after his return to England, murdered his father, and the pictures he painted at Broadmoor have retained a pathetic and macabre interest and are occasionally exhibited. The rest of the tourists, with one exception, have disappeared.

The exception was the youngest of the visitors. Mansfield Parkyns was only nineteen years old when he arrived in Egypt in December 1842. He had recently been obliged to leave Trinity College, Cambridge, without a degree, less than a year after his matriculation. Naturally, this had been a disappointment, although it was some consolation to him that he could turn to travel and the study of natural history as alternatives to the university's mild discipline against which he had offended.

While loitering on the Nile, Mansfield Parkyns declared his real interests when he observed that 'he would rather find a new and beautiful butterfly than see the most gigantic and glorious works of human genius and skill'. It was a remark that was boyishly facetious and in keeping with his appearance and style, for there was an air about him of independence: an unhappy freedom from parents because both of them were dead; his class's freedom from official regulation; no lack of money and a heedlessness of convention when it became a hindrance. Yet Parkyns won this notable tribute from Sir

Francis Galton in his autobiography: 'of the many travellers whom I have known I should place Mansfield Parkyns as perhaps the most gifted with natural advantages for that career'. An opinion of this kind from Galton carries weight, for it was generally conceded that his approbation had to be earned and that he had an especially close acquaintance with the travellers of the great period of nineteenth-century exploration. He knew them all. He himself was a gold medallist of the Royal Geographical Society for his explorations in South West Africa, and he was the society's honorary secretary for several years. His term as a member of the society's council extended to nearly forty years, from 1854 to 1893. Moreover, he was author of a book, *Art of Travel; or, Shifts and Contrivances in Wild Countries* – the forerunner of *Hints to Travellers* – which was considered essential reading for every visitor to remote places. The person most quoted as a source of 'shifts and contrivances' was Mansfield Parkyns.

What were the qualities that made Parkyns such a notable traveller? What were the circumstances in which he was able to display these qualities? From whence they derived? And why has he received so little recognition? These are the questions I hope to answer in this book.

I

Outwardly, Mansfield Parkyns was conventional enough. He was a good-looking, compact and athletic young man with the offhand, self-deprecatory air of English amateurism. Some people, although not many at the time, found this affectation irritating, quite rightly believing that it expressed, too assertively, the confidence of a privileged class that need not lay claim upon the merits of the individual. They would have been wrong, however, if they supposed that conventional manners obliterated individuality, or if they dismissed individual taste and conviction as mere eccentricity. Members of the Parkyns family, for several generations, had given their acquaintances reason to ponder the proposition.

On his father's side, Harry Mansfield Isham Parkyns came from a Nottinghamshire family that had made its mark in local affairs. A succession of Parkynses represented Nottingham in Parliament and several held the office of High Sheriff of the county that included Sherwood Forest. Generation after generation included men and women of varied talents. It was also a family in which good looks, if not outstanding beauty, were repeated, and are to be admired today, long after the male line has ended.

In Nottinghamshire, the fortunes of the family went back to a lawyer – Richard Parkyns, of ancient Worcestershire and Berkshire stock – who, in the days of the first Elizabeth, after becoming Recorder for Nottingham, married the widow of the lord of the manor of Boney, or Bunny as it is now known, a few miles south of the city and not far from the county boundary with Leicestershire. This was the beginning of broad acres for the Parkyns family and the end of the freehold yeomen whose acres they purchased. It was the beginning of honours too, for during the English Civil War it was a Parkyns – Colonel Isham Parkyns – who was the last to surrender a royalist stronghold. In recognition of his defence of Ashby de la Zouch, Charles II bestowed a baronetcy on Colonel Isham's son.

Perhaps the best remembered personality in the family was the first baronet's heir who lived from 1662 to 1741. By profession, Sir Thomas Parkyns was a barrister; but he did not practice at the bar after marrying a Nottinghamshire heiress. Instead, he devoted his energies to developing his property, an activity to which he brought the skills of an intelligent farmer together with those of an inventive architect and builder.

In many respects, there was little to distinguish Sir Thomas from other wealthy squires of his time, except that he was a promoter of the modern sport of wrestling and a practising wrestler himself. In 1734, he published the results of his study of the subject in a book: *The Inn Play: or Cornish Hugg Wrestler. Digested in a method that teacheth to break all holds and throw most falls mathematically.* Annual tournaments were held at Bunny to which even wrestlers from Cornwall made their way in the hope of winning the first prize of two guineas and a laced hat.

Sir Thomas lived to the age of seventy-eight and his muscular hobby followed him to the grave, for he is commemorated by a memorial in Bunny Church on which his effigy stands four-square with arms extended ready for a 'hugg'. Some clergymen thought the memorial too explicit, and inappropriate for a church, but most people felt that special recognition was needed for a man of whom it was said that 'he could throw a tenant, combat a paradox, or quote Martial, or sign a mittimus with any man of his own age or country'. The Latin epitaph on the memorial was construed by a vicar of Bunny to read:

Here lies a man famous in the British ring
Whom thou has just thrown in a long match, O Time;

Hence he flies for the first time thrown; except Thee, he had conquered all;
Over Thee too he will be victorious when he rises again.

He was long remembered with awe and a certain affection in his neighbourhood; not least because the strain of originality in the Parkyns family found less engaging outlets in the two generations that followed him. His son, Sir Thomas Parkyns, the 3rd baronet and Mansfield Parkyns' grandfather, complicated the family tree by his three marriages. First, he married his great-niece of the half blood; an alliance that created some speculation. Secondly, he married one of his housemaids, and thirdly, at the age of sixty-eight, his children's nurse whose son was Mansfield Parkyns' father.

The next in line was another Thomas Parkyns, who never succeeded to the Parkyns baronetcy because he was outlived by his father. Moreover, his service in the Army and at court, removed him from the close connection with Nottinghamshire affairs that had been characteristic of his forebears. Instead, he acquired influential friends and was drawn into the dissolute and spendthrift set that surrounded the Prince of Wales (the future Prince Regent and King George IV). First, he became an equerry at court, and then he was given command, in 1795, of a fashionable militia regiment; the Prince of Wales Fencibles, a formation better known for its uniforms than its battle-honours. His reward was the barony of Rancliffe in the Irish peerage, but the pace had been hot and he died in 1800 at the age of forty-five.

Colonel Parkyns, before he became Lord Rancliffe, had prudently married the only daughter of an Indian nabob, Sir William James of Eltham Park in Kent. She was a girl of great wealth and extravagance, whose eldest son George was the godson of the Prince Regent. The Rancliffe peerage and what remained of the nabob's fortune came to him at the age of fifteen and, in 1806, he succeeded his grandfather as the 4th Parkyns baronet at the age of twenty-one when his unencumbered income was estimated to be about £21,000 per annum. With legacies of this kind, and the minimum of discipline and restraint during his boyhood, it is hardly surprising that George Rancliffe should have grown into a caricature of Regency manhood who participated in most extravagances of contemporary behaviour. All agreed that he had charming manners and that he was a superb horseman, accomplishments that his relations did not regard as adequate compensation for his spiteful conduct towards them. When he died in 1850 without children, he ignored his Parkyns relations and left the whole of his property, including the Bunny estates, to his mistress, the wife of the local doctor.

Mansfield Parkyns was Lord Rancliffe's cousin of the half blood, although thirty years his junior, and he was born at Caen in Normandy in February 1823 while his parents were on one of their visits to the Continent. His father was not on good terms with Lord Rancliffe; his health was indifferent and he preferred to live on the fringe of the international society that wandered over Europe in the years that followed the Congress of Vienna. As a result Mansfield and his older brother Tom, the heir to the Parkyns baronetcy, led a peripatetic life; sometimes at the South Manor at Ruddington, three miles from Bunny Park on the Nottingham road; sometimes at a house belonging to his mother at Newland in the Forest of Dean; and sometimes abroad, particularly in Italy where his father died in 1833 when Mansfield was ten years old.

From this brief indication of his Parkyns forebears, one is justified in concluding that Mansfield emerged from an English 'aristocratic' tradition of the raffish and red-blooded variety; but his heritage from his mother's family was different and, since his father died when he was young, one may suppose that it was a substantial influence.

His mother was born Charlotte Smith of Edwalton, a village near Nottingham. She was a granddaughter of Abel Smith, the eighteenth-century Nottingham merchant and banker whose progeny was numerous and capable, nurtured in the commercial tradition of English society. However, by the time Charlotte Smith married into the Parkyns family the characteristics and social status of the Abel Smiths had been modified by marriage and wealth. For many years they provided Members of Parliament for Nottingham, often in opposition to candidates from Bunny Park. Later in the century, as many as five of these Smiths sat in the same Parliament, and other Smiths, the Lords Carrington, Bicester and Pauncefoot, have sat in the House of Lords. However, their commercial skills were undiminished and Mansfield Parkyns would have had fewer worries in life if he had inherited a better share of them. Instead, he had wealthy Smith relations, some of them fairly distant, to be found in mansions throughout the English countryside; for example, East Stoke on the Trent, Woodhall Park in Hertfordshire, Wycombe Abbey in Buckinghamshire, Shottesbrook Park in Berkshire, Tresco Abbey in the Isles of Scilly. One of their memorials is the contribution they made to the emergence of what is now the National Westminster Bank through their Nottingham bank of Smith, Payne and Smiths; and there were many other enterprises. Clearly, his Smith relations could demonstrate to Mansfield that there was an alternative to the Parkyns view of life; an obvious difference being that the Smiths were climbing the ladder of influence as steadily as the Parkyns family was slipping down it.

If Mansfield Parkyns were aware of this, and there is no evidence one way or the other, his character was not influenced by a feeling of resentful defiance. On the contrary, he accepted life and his comfortable position in it as he found it, claiming that he was 'careless and easily satisfied'. He was also blessed with genuine modesty.

For a boy who loved country life and who also happened to bear the name of Parkyns in Nottinghamshire, the years immediately preceding Queen Victoria's accession were splendid ones in which to grow up. A boy of Mansfield's age could not be expected to be concerned with the urban enormities of the Industrial Revolution, although they were evident enough in Nottingham, and even in Ruddington where the stocking-knitting cottagers took violent action. At least half England's population still lived and worked in the countryside, and most of them believed that they belonged to the wealthiest, the most energetic, and the most free community in the world.

From the evidence of the tastes that Mansfield Parkyns acquired as a boy, one can see that his education was provided by more than his parents and tutors. Although he grew up in a period when parents knew what was good for their children, and formal education was not left to a schoolboy's whim, he learned most of the things he enjoyed from country people; particularly from those among them who could satisfy his love of wildlife. His mentors are recognizable from William Hewitt's description:

[5]

They affect fustian or velveteen jackets with wide skirts and huge pockets; gaiters and strong shoes. They have a lounging, yet unauthorised air and they have always some excuse for enjoying a gun; they are stuffers of curious birds and animals . . . some are incorrigible poachers, from the love of the pursuit of wild creatures, of strolling about in solitary glens and woods, of night-watching, and adventures . . . Happy is the man of this stamp who reaches America. That is the land for him! There he may roam the paradise of back settlements, and satiate his soul with lying in wait, and with wild adventure, without fear of game-laws.

By the age of nineteen Mansfield Parkyns, with mentors of this kind, was an exceptionally fine shot, an informed ornithologist, a competent taxidermist, a formidable boxer and he once admitted that 'I used to be celebrated as a boy at singlesticks' (fencing with sticks); the only reference he ever made to his accomplishments. If his friends the poachers-turned-keepers were well qualified to become frontiersmen in America, they also taught Mansfield Parkyns what would be useful to him for studying *terra incognita* in Africa.

In the meantime, he had to undergo more formal education and develop his talent for drawing and painting. With his penchant for open-air pursuits and sports it was unlikely that he would find life in an educational institution anything but irksome.

In September 1833 Mansfield Parkyns, at the age of ten and a half, was parted from the comfortable home at Ruddington and driven through the Leicestershire countryside to the grammar school at Uppingham in Rutland. His elder brother Tom, the heir to the Parkyns baronetcy, went to Eton; a conventional discrimination.

At the time, Thomas Hughes was at Rugby, thirty miles away, observing the scene that led to his writing *Tom Brown's Schooldays*; but Dr Arnold's influence had not yet reached Uppingham and it was not until twenty years later that Dr Thring arrived to give the school its educational reputation under his headmastership. When Mansfield was there things were different, for there were only some twenty-five pupils and the school was overdue for reform. Indeed, one wonders what conditions were really like before Dr Thring's civilizing regime when one reads a tribute to him by one of his admiring pupils. 'Uppingham?', he wrote, 'That's Dr. Thring's school, where they whip the boys so . . . He has no modern humanitarian taint in him.'

What did Mansfield Parkyns think of his experiences? Some years later he remarked that 'beyond the ordinary complaints of childhood and many a sound and well-deserved whipping at school, I led a life of sunshine'. The hedgerows of Rutland and the watermeadows of the Ouse were to his taste. As he put it, 'everything was fair in the open air'.

He was not long at Uppingham for his mother remarried and he was sent to a tutor at Woolwich who was associated in some way with 'the Shop', or Royal Military Academy. Why he transferred to Trinity College, Cambridge, instead of going on to the Shop is not known. He matriculated as a pensioner at Trinity in the Michaelmas term of 1840. That he read mathematics was an indication that his education was not to be entirely frivolous; sufficient perhaps to fit him for a position in one of the Smith banks. In the unreformed university, this was one of the ways by which an undergraduate could proceed to an honours degree. Mathematics continued to interest him and in the remote places he subsequently visited he amused himself by solving quite complicated mathematical problems. Nor was Parkyns ignorant of Latin, for he mustered a good choice of tags when needed.

His mother died in 1838, and one supposes that he looked forward to communal life at Trinity, a college with which the Parkyns family had been associated continuously since Tudor times. Trinity offered splendid opportunities for a young man of Mansfield's spirit. Even if his boyhood tastes were not close to those of the university's academic core, he was no anti-intellectual in the aggressive early Victorian sense. He simply did not regard himself as possessing intellectual qualities, a feeling he shared with a fair proportion of his fellow-undergraduates.

Perhaps young Mansfield was not the kind of undergraduate to appeal to Dr Christopher Wordsworth, the poet's younger brother, who was ending his career as Master of Trinity; a misanthropic widower nearly seventy years old, and a disciplinarian who demanded conformity to college rules. This he was unlikely to get from Mansfield Parkyns who was a high-spirited, imaginative and harmless nonconformist. Perhaps it is not surprising that Parkyns was obliged to leave Trinity within a year. There is no record in the Conclusions Book of the college that he was sent down. Probably his guardian was asked to remove him. Many years later, one of his daughters said that he had done nothing worse than paint and dress up some statues in one of the courts at Trinity; a story that sounds *ben trovato*. A contemporary at Trinity – Francis Galton – in an unpublished journal, wrote that Parkyns had 'taken part in an unfortunate row and found it best to leave', while, in his published autobiography, he mentioned the incident as 'a Cambridge scrape'. It cannot have been a particularly heinous offence.

Mansfield never mentioned his departure from Cambridge in anything he wrote, although it is significant that he should have made a comparison between a village brawl in Abyssinia and a Cambridge 'town and gown' riot, being familiar with both. The abrupt termination of his education may have been the cause of his lack of confidence in his own abilities, other than physical, that dogged him for the rest of his life. Years later, he declared himself to be 'little gifted and half savage by education', an exaggerated self-criticism.

At eighteen, he was light-hearted, friendly and rather facetious; given to using Sam Weller's argot, in the fashion of the time, when reciting anecdotes. To him, trousers were 'inexpressibles' and Africans 'niggers', following the respectable example of Thomas Carlyle and most of his contemporaries. On the other hand, he would soon demonstrate that he could dispense with 'inexpressibles' and live on the friendliest terms with Africans in a manner that was far from conventional in his day. Also he developed prejudices. Modest himself – suffering from a sense of inferiority, some might think – he disliked and distrusted hubris in others.

However, in the Parkyns tradition, Mansfield was not much inclined to intellectual speculation, nor, in the Smith tradition, to over-long contemplation of problems before making up his mind. Above all, he was young and disappointed by his rebuff at Cambridge, yet brimming with eagerness to test his body and his will against his many-sided curiosity. The question was, in which direction could his energies be best employed?

Given his inclinations and background, the question was

easily answered. He would go abroad. It is unlikely that his elders attached much importance to his dismissal from Cambridge. All would agree that a tour of the Continent was an appropriate way for him to spend his time while it was decided what he should do next. They could not know that many years were to pass before they would see him again nor that they would be led to conclude that he had lost his life.

Exactly when and where Mansfield Parkyns decided to join in the search for the sources of the White Nile and, if possible, to cross Africa from the Red Sea to the Atlantic is not known. It was not an original idea, for other young men had used these aims as excuses for wandering into darkest Africa in search of adventure and fame. However, it is unlikely that Parkyns was influenced by a desire for fame, that is to say, by a determination to be the first European to cross the continent. Probably nothing was farther from his mind. Had he any motive other than his conventional claim that he wished to visit fresh fields for the study of natural history? We do not know. Perhaps he wanted to explore his own heart as much as the heart of Africa. If this were so, his attitude is more understandable today than it was to his contemporaries in early Victorian times.

In any case, an informal walk across Africa was not the sort of project to be taken seriously by the Royal Geographical Society. The aim of the Society was to promote disciplined scientific exploration, and its council wished to ensure that, if an explorer reached his objective, he should not waste his time there for lack of knowledge of what information to collect. The Society's *Hints to Travellers* had not yet been published, but anyone who sought its advice in 1842 could expect to be given a list of over a hundred questions to which answers were thought to be necessary, in addition to standard requests for astronomical fixes, compass traverses, altitudes, anthropological, geological and meterological data. The Society's secretary, Colonel Julian Jackson, had published in 1841 a book of 515 pages entitled *What to Observe, or the Travellers Rememberencer*. The seventy items under 'Operations' ranged from how 'to walk in a straight line', and how 'to collect the gases from volcanoes' to 'How to climb trees' and how 'to map a country'.

Parkyns did not consult the RGS and there is no indication that he had anything so thorough in mind.

It was probably the prospect of finding and collecting specimens of outlandish birds, animals and insects that tempted him
most. When he left England, he told no one of his African plan.

Parkyns was no simpleton despite his failure at Cambridge.
He was good at languages and, if his style was casual, his
intelligence was far from negligible. Also, he had talent as an
artist and he could write effectively when he tried. He had an
inquiring mind and a willingness to experiment. For example,
at one stage in his travels, while describing an unnecessary
diversion from his route, he explained:

> The object I had in mind was not that I expected to see
> anything particularly curious or interesting . . . but that it
> was a new and not very easy route, and these two motives are
> in general sufficient to tempt a traveller anywhere.

It was a comment that had a ring of truth that other travellers
would probably recognize even if their editors would not
approve their saying so in writing. They preferred their
travellers to be more serious.

Parkyns was not totally ignorant of what was involved in the
plan he had in mind. Most country houses had atlases and
globes in their libraries, as well as the standard works of earlier
travellers. No doubt he had seen an edition of James Bruce's
Travels and we know that one source of his interest in natural
history was Charles Waterton. Most schoolboys at the time,
including Hughes's *Tom Brown*, read Waterton's books with
almost as much enjoyment as they obtained from the instal-
ments of *Pickwick Papers* that were appearing monthly when
Mansfield was at school. Of particular appeal to him were the
last twenty pages of Waterton's *Wanderings in South America*
which contained valuable instructions on taxidermy, and particularly on the collection and preparation of specimens in the
field.

Above all, a reader of Waterton's travels would be reassured
that ponderous arrangements for going to remote places were
not the necessity that the accounts of some explorers might
suggest. Yet there was nothing primitive about the arrangements Parkyns made when he travelled through Europe in
1842. He was in no hurry and he went as an ordinary well-to-do
tourist with congenial companions and the occasional help of
early railways and steamships. After visits to Switzerland and

Italy, he arrived in Greece in the late summer and then decided to go on to the Levant. If he had Waterton's experiences in mind, his progress must have seemed too conventional; but for Parkyns, 'Waterton' was a book, and not a person. Sooner or later, a person must replace the schoolboys, stableboys, fencing masters and undergraduates who, apart from his family and tutor, had filled his life. What he needed was the acquaintance of someone who could develop his lively mind.

It was by a singular chance, therefore, that Parkyns, after leaving Greece, should have come across a man who could give him a version of the civilizing influences he needed and, at the same time, show him friendship and understanding. The meeting occurred at Syra, the principal island of the Cyclades in the Aegean, where the early steamer services from the French and Italian ports used to call on their way to the Levant. There, Richard Monckton Milnes was waiting for a paddle-steamer to take him to Istanbul and he sailed with Parkyns and his friends to the Ottoman capital. From there, like Parkyns, he intended to visit Egypt and he invited Parkyns to accompany him.

Richard Milnes was thirteen years older than Parkyns. He was a member of parliament, a minor poet and a cosmopolitan with a wide range of influential friends. On the face of it, all the two men had in common was that both had been at Trinity College, Cambridge, and both were the sons of Midland squires. Even in their attitudes to country life their tastes differed. Parkyns revelled in country pursuits; Milnes detested them. As for their respective careers at Cambridge, there could hardly have been a greater contrast. Parkyns, the high-spirited 'blood', had not completed his first year before he was removed. In Milnes' first year he had been chosen to be one of the so-called 'apostles', the name given to the members of the Conversazione Society, usually regarded as academically the most astringent and exclusive society for self-conscious intellectuals in the university. Among his contemporaries and acquaintances at Trinity – some of them close friends – were literary figures of repute: Tennyson, Hallam, Thackeray, Kinglake and Eliot Warburton. Together they savoured the last years of the Georgian period at Trinity, the 'dawn-golden times' of Tennyson's *In Memoriam*.

Even in this company Milnes' literary future seemed assured; but he also had political ambitions and he seems to have assumed that these would prosper equally. Unhappily for Milnes this was not to be. A year before his visit to Egypt, he had experienced his first reverse by failing to be chosen for the post of under-secretary of state for foreign affairs when Peel's Tory administration took office in 1841. For a place in the cabinet, on this occasion, the competition was severe. Out of fifteen members, seven had been, or were destined to be, prime ministers and five of them viceroys of India. Milnes' lack of success was hardly surprising to his contemporaries. He was an unconvincing Tory who commented that 'it is certainly easier to be a free-minded and unselfish liberal than a Tory'. Crossing the floor of the house in 1846 to join the Liberals brought him a peerage in 1863, as Lord Houghton, but never a place in the cabinet.

Milnes' manner was not to everyone's taste. Thomas Carlyle described him to Emerson as an 'Italianized little man . . . a dimple, next to no chin, and he flings his arm around your neck when he addresses you in public society'. Thackeray called him 'Miss Nancy' and said that nothing irritated him more than to see Milnes strive to get into the orbit of some great man; Sidney Smith went out of his way to assure Milnes that he was not responsible for nicknames he resented, for example, 'In-I-go Jones', 'London Assurance' and 'Cool-of-the-evening'; Disraeli could not stand him – describing Milnes' poor showing in debate, he commented that 'though he might be descanting on the wrongs of Poland or the rights of Italy, there was sure to be a laugh' – and he once wrote that Milnes had a face 'like a Herculaneum mask, or a countenance cut out of an orange'. Nor could many Victorians who were aware of it forgive his reputation as a sensualist, and even less his preoccupation with his library of pornography. The fact that he was not hypocritical about these predilections made them seem all the worse.

Mansfield Parkyns would not appear to have been a promising target for moral corruption, if that is what Milnes had in mind. Many of his contemporaries might have assumed that he had but there is no evidence to support such a belief. As his biographer has shown, Milnes' reputation suffered as much from Victorian prudery as it did from his own tastes. He was, in fact, a man of strong intellect, with a generous heart and a practical attitude to humanitarian reform in general and the needs of deserving writers and artists in particular. Not least,

[12]

he was a good companion, 'gregarious, and full of conversation and gossip', with a gift for getting on well with, and getting the best out of, unusual characters.

Perhaps Milnes and Parkyns were not such an incongruous pair after all. At the time, Milnes needed companionship, or at least an audience. As his biographer – James Pope-Hennesy – points out, Milnes 'preferred the company of high spirited eccentrics to any other' and perhaps in Mansfield Parkyns he found some of the characteristics that entertained him.

Parkyns himself could only benefit from association with a man of intellect and knowledge of public affairs. Moreover it says much for him that he valued the experience. Most young men of his stamp would have found Milnes intolerable. Parkyns was respectful of Milnes' seniority and status, but otherwise uninhibited in dealing with him. From references in his letters to subjects they discussed when they were together, it is evident that he found Milnes' active mind stimulating rather than oppressive. By the time their steamer paddled her way round the Seraglio Point into the bay of the Golden Horn at Constantinople a friendship was established. Parkyns and Milnes settled into the Hôtel d'Angleterre across the bay in Pera, better known as Missirie's Hotel after its proprietor, James Missirie, who had been Alexander Kinglake's dragoman – interpreter and general factotum – during the tour, seven years earlier, that he described in *Eothen*, an early Victorian 'best seller'.

From Parkyns' point of view, and with more exciting prospects ahead, this visit to Istanbul seemed rather a waste of time. He was not much interested in antiquities except as subjects for drawing. All he had to say was: 'We had a pleasant party at Missirie's Hotel, and made many interesting visits to the mosques, seraglios, and dervishes, both howlers and dancers'. He disliked cities, whatever their nationality: 'In all capitals,' he wrote, 'I feel out of my element, losing at once my health, spirits, and all the little disposition and energy for work I may possess'. City dwellers he regarded as countrymen who had lost their way.

For Richard Milnes capitals were places where important people lived and he lost no time in riding out on the hills above the Bosporus to the country residence of Sir Stratford Canning, whose embassy at Pera had been destroyed recently by fire (a

fairly regular occurrence). The formidable ambassador, recently one of Milnes' colleagues at Westminster, had returned
to Istanbul early in 1842 to a post that he first occupied during
the Napoleonic Wars at the age of twenty-four and did not
finally relinquish until he was seventy-two. He was prepared to
speak with authority on any subject connected with the Ottoman realm. Milnes felt that he needed a better understanding
of Turks, their empire and the Muslim religion; at least, a
better understanding than the one Dickens attributed to Mrs
Skewton: 'Say, like those wicked Turks, there is no What's-his-
name but Thingummy, and What-you-may-call-it is his
prophet!' It was not too severe a caricature of popular knowledge of these matters in England at the time. Public opinion of
the Turks was influenced less by informed literature than by
stories of the treatment of sailors captured by Barbary pirates,
and by the villainous figures of scimitar-bearing janissaries sold
with the 'penny theatres'.

It was arranged for Milnes to meet Sami Effendi, who had
been sent to Istanbul by Muhammed Ali Pasha, the governor of
the Sultan's Egyptian province, as his negotiator. Milnes had
suffered some discomfort in the recent crisis in the Eastern
Question as a result of his incorrect information about the
relationship between the Pasha and the Sublime Porte, the
government of the Ottoman Empire. Apart from having questions about this, he wanted to assess the prospects for the
reform of the Ottoman realm and its institutions, reform to
which liberal-minded politicians in England were giving hope-
ful support. His experiences with Sami Effendi were not en-
couraging. Rather than answer embarrassing questions. Sami
Effendi preferred to impress his visitor with his knowledge of
European customs and practices. Reform for him meant
strengthening the bureaucracy, of which he was a part, to his
own advantage. To his credit, Milnes admitted in his preface to
his book of verse, *Palm Leaves*, that he had failed to achieve the
understanding he sought 'for one decisive consideration – I
knew nothing of the languages of the countries I was visiting'.
Nor did the literary friends who followed in his steps – W.M.
Thackeray and Eliot Warburton – but they did not draw
attention to their handicap.

The interlude in the capital was not all as serious as this, for
there were young acquaintances at the British embassy who

arranged for the visitors' entertainment and, before long, stories were circulating in Pall Mall about the adventures of Milnes and his friends among the odalisques and dancing girls on the shores of the Bosporus. Nevertheless, their visit was not an entire waste of time. For Parkyns, intent on travelling to the limits of the Ottoman realm, it was well for him to see, before going to Cairo, the hub of an empire. Ramshackle it might now appear to European eyes but it had been greatly feared in the not-too-distant past, and was to survive longer than expected.

When the time came for Milnes and Parkyns to leave for Egypt, Parkyns decided to ride overland to infidel Smyrna, while Milnes went by sea. He thoroughly enjoyed a nine-day excursion through the Troad and Bergama, watching the birds, basking in the sun, trying to talk to the country people and viewing the scenery with a painter's eye. It was a welcome contrast to the city. He wrote:

> The colourings of the foregrounds were brilliant in the extreme. Rocks of the richest red and yellow ochres contrasted well with the green dark foliage of the pine and the autumnal orange of the walloneel oak. In places, a smooth turf slope leading down to a rivulet, would give the scene the appearance of a park, while from every elevation the beautiful island of Tenedos and the Archipelago were seen blue in the distance.

One can understand why, at the age of nineteen, the pleasures of travel without the help of the wheel exceeded its toils. This was only a first taste of it.

2

Parkyns rejoined Milnes and the two men set off by another
steamer for Egypt. They were to land at Alexandria in sight of
the remains of the Greek and Roman occupations that figured
largely in their classical educations. In the event there was not
much to see. Modern Alexandrians were most interested in
pursuing their imitations of modern Europe than in the crumb-
ling foundations of buildings bearing unfamiliar classical
names. According to a contemporary and excessively flattering
description of the Grande Place: 'The houses are built as
regularly as Park Crescent, and two stories high above the
porte-cochere. It might be a fashionable watering-place in England or France.' Before long, one of the principal British
merchants would build a villa beyond the Grande Place with a
name-plate reminiscent of London's suburbia – The Sycamores.

All Parkyns had to say about Alexandria, then in the early
stages of its modern reconstruction, was that its appearance 'is
highly interesting to a man who delights in commerce, or whose
heart gladdens as he sees an embryo Europe about to be
hatched in Africa'. Clearly it did not gladden young Parkyns'
heart, shocking as this might be to some of his Smith relations.

Parkyns was glad to embark for Cairo, and sail along the
winding Maymudiyah Canal to the Nile. Here he and Milnes
boarded the small paddle-steamer operated as part of the

overload route between the Mediterranean and the Red Sea. On the following morning, as the *Jack o'Lantern* thrashed her way up a broad reach of the Nile, Parkyns and Milnes had their first sight of Cairo, luminous in the early light with the thin white smoke of the morning fires drifting over it.

The turbulent arrival at Boulak, Cairo's main riverside quay, was familiar to all European travellers as their awkward baggage was disembarked and loaded on camels for transport to the city. They themselves trotted on donkeys towards the city walls in sunlight and dust. They followed a mile of road that General Bonaparte had made forty years earlier; past clay warehouses and dwellings; past dust-laden sycamores and over primitive bridges spanning two empty canals; past people and animals, moving and dormant, and sometimes dead. This was where the travellers whose books Parkyns' had read had made their start; where the more serious of them spent months learning Arabic and collecting information before they embarked on their expeditions. Parkyns had no intention of following their example, but he would learn what he could. He knew that it had all been described dozens of times and he did not think it necessary to add impressions of his own. The city still had the atmosphere of a capital, with decaying legacies of art and fancy from civilizations that flourished when Europe was a wilderness, but change was in progress both in the city and in the Europeans who observed it. Later in 1843 Eliot Warburton still saw the crowds in Cairo's narrow streets as the '*dramatis personae* of the Arabian Nights'. To him, the horizon of Cairo was 'like a dream, or a sea of minarets and palm-tree tops, with the domes of mosques like great gilt and turquoise bubbles protruding above the houses'. A few years later, Gustave Flaubert saw the people as: 'Scoundrels in gold-braided rags, and covered with vermin . . . among the perfume of lime-bushes and the stench of corpses'. The camera had not yet intruded as arbiter between the romantic and the realist. Some years were to pass before Cairo earned its classic nineteenth-century description as 'a fading Arabian Nights and still-born Rue de Rivoli'.

A visiting European in the days of Muhammed Ali Pasha's rule had no difficulty in recognizing the impact of modern Europe on the city of Cairo, although he might find difficulty in placing it in rational historical perspective. However, his main concern was likely to be his physical comfort, and in this direction there had been improvements. The increasing number of passengers using the overland route to and from India had made 'hotels', more or less in the European style, a necessity in Cairo. In December 1842 the new Hôtel d'Orient, with sixty rooms, on the Ezbekiya Square, had not yet opened its doors and Parkyns stayed at a more traditional hostelry belonging to J. R. Hill & Co, agents for P & O. It could not be missed because travellers entering the Ezbekiya Square were confronted, on the far side, by a signboard in English pointing down a side-street to the Grand Eastern Hotel; an infidel innovation in a converted Mameluke house.

Richard Milnes' first engagement was an interview with Muhammed Ali Pasha, the Turkish governor of Egypt, who for almost forty years had given the country a state of order it had not experienced for a long time. There was no difficulty about arranging the meeting because Milnes was carrying a letter of introduction to the Pasha's Armenian secretary which underlined the sympathetic attitude he had taken to the Pasha's cause during his recent contest with the Sultan. So Milnes was soon riding out to the Pasha's pleasance on the Nile where Italian architects, imported from Constantinople, had built him a retreat befitting a Turkish Pasha's taste in the early Ottoman-Rothschild manner.

It was quiet. It had an air of opulence. The odour of damp earth and limes rose from the garden, and the sound of running water – essential to Turkish luxury – was provided by jets of water that splashed into a marble pool from the jaws of marble crocodiles.

The ageing, white-bearded Turk of Albanian origin was not an entirely spent force in spite of his enforced withdrawal from Syria and Arabia. It was a tribute to his skill and determination that most Europeans regarded his tyrannical methods as evidence of enlightenment, although some well-informed contemporaries suspected he was more strongly motivated by fear of revenge at the hands of those in Istanbul whom he had offended during his rise to power. Being excluded from the Levant by the Treaty of London, henceforth his acquisitive energies would have to be satisfied in the part of Africa south of the Sahara to which the Nile gives convenient access from Egypt.

In the meantime Parkyns was confined to the hotel by the

kind of intestinal upset that Europeans expected to experience in Egypt. He had not the least interest in pashas and prime ministers, except to keep out of their way and to trust that they did not exercise their powers to his detriment. He was still no more than Richard Monckton Milnes' unconsidered young companion, but he was never bored with his own company and hobbies, even when he was waiting for escape from a city into less confining spaces. On this occasion in Cairo his indisposition was not a bad thing because it gave him a better opportunity for meeting callers at the hotel who talked about unexplored places south of the Sahara and particularly Abyssinia, where his journey would commence.

For Europeans at this time, nine-tenths of inner Africa was *terra incognita*. A contemporary geographical textbook pronounced: 'Africa is a country of monsters. Every species of noxious and predatory animal reigns undisturbed in the vast deserts of this continent.' In East Africa no European had yet seen Mount Kenya or the great equatorial lakes. Yet the name 'Abyssinia' was familiar to well-read people.

They would have known of the 'Aethiopea' of the Bible; of the legends of Prestor John and his Christian empire isolated beyond the Islamic barriers; of the exploits there of the Portuguese and Jesuit missionaries in the country during the sixteenth and seventeenth centuries; of Samuel Johnson's *Rasselas*; of James Bruce's journey to the source of the Blue Nile and his outrageous reminiscences. More recently Henry Salt had published his accounts of his visits to the country in 1805 and 1810, embellished with pictures of scenery and monuments.

Yet the response, even of educated readers, to all this information often reflected the preoccupations and prejudices of their own society rather than any true understanding of the people they read about. After consulting these authorities, Macauley, the Victorian historian, concluded that the Abyssinians were 'filthy savages, ignorant of their letters, and gorged with raw steaks from living cows', and that they lived in 'a land of harems, a land of polygamy, a land where women were married without ever being seen . . . where there is boundless liberty of divorce'.

Although the number of Western European residents in Cairo in those days was small many had first-hand experience of Abyssinia. They used Mr Raven, the manager's, office or 'snuggery' as he called it, at the hotel, almost as a club where they could gossip, read the news from Europe in *Galignani's Messenger*, drink coffee, smoke their Manila cigars, and impress travellers staying at the hotel with their knowledge of local affairs. Among them was Dr Henry Abbott, a vast man in Turkish dress who wore on his finger a large golden ring which, he explained, had been worn previously by Cheops, the supposed builder of the Great Pyramid. Dr Abbott had once visited the coast of Abyssinia, and was regarded as an authority on the exploration of the country in which a number of his French acquaintances in Cairo had been taking part.

There were others. For example, the Pasha's capable French engineer, Adolphe Linant de Bellefonds, who, with assistance from the Royal Geographical Society, had travelled extensively in the remoter parts of the Pasha's southern possessions, and who had sailed one hundred and fifty miles up the White Nile from Khartoum as early as 1827, when Parkyns was still an infant. He was by far the most accomplished geographer in Egypt. All must have regarded the feckless Parkyns quizzically, for they had seen a number of young men with Parkyns' ambition to cross the continent to the Atlantic set off for Equatorial Africa never to return.

Parkyns was not to be deterred. From Cairo, he wrote to London ordering the instruments and other supplies and equipment he thought he would need. Apparently, he made his decision after meeting a young man, John Bell, who was staying with Dr Abbott at his Arab mansion while recuperating from a spear wound sustained in the highlands of northern Abyssinia. The tale of his adventures was nicely calculated to arouse the younger traveller's interest.

John Bell had been born in Malta, the son of a master mariner from Bristol. He had come to Cairo in 1837 to work for Lieutenant Waghorn, the organizer of the overland route across Egypt from the Mediterranean to the Red Sea. Three years later he volunteered to undertake a search for a young Englishman called Airston who had disappeared in Abyssinia. On arrival Bell found that young Mr Airston was dead, but instead of returning to Cairo he made his way up the escarpment to the traditional capital of Gondar and thence to the Galla highlands where he believed the source of the White Nile might be hidden. Beyond Gondar, on the east side of Lake Tana, he was attacked by bandits and there received a spear wound in the face so severe that most of his companions, supposing him dead, abandoned him.

Bell, however, recovered consciousness. He later wrote:

> The ground near the spot was covered with blood, and it was with the greatest difficulty that we managed to reach Corata, on Lake Tana, which was about half an hour's walk from where we were attacked . . . We succeeded in reaching the church, at the door of which we sank exhausted and unable to move; fortunately for us Ayto Cassai, a merchant whom I had known at Massawa, came up at the moment and kindly had us taken to his house . . . All the ladies of the family came to render us what assistance they could; and first, brought us a drinking horn filled with a sort of beer, which I endeavoured to drink, but to my astonishment much of it came through the wound between my eyes, having as I suppose, found its way through the aperture made by the lance in the palette of my mouth, and caused me excruciating pain.

Miraculously, this wound did not kill Bell. Before it was fully healed, and carrying in a little leather bag round his neck some of the bones that had been removed from the roof of his mouth, he attached himself to the train of Ras Oubie, one of the local rulers. For the following year Bell followed his new patron through a confused and sporadic campaign that was part of a larger struggle to wrest power from the country's failing monarchy.

Bell was equipped with a good mule, two lances, and 'a very handsome shield beautifully ornamented in gold and silver, with the mane and tail of a lion'. Towards the end of 1842 he appeared in Aden still wearing Abyssinian dress, with his shoulders uncovered, to the scandal of at least one English visitor. He was on his way to Cairo to recuperate his health under Dr Abbott's care. A correspondent later informed the Royal Geographical Society that Mr Bell was 'tall, strong and intelligent' but 'perfectly careless'.

Certainly, his experiences had not deterred Bell from returning to Abyssinia. On the contrary, he was about to make another attempt to reach the White Nile, and it seems likely that he was seeking in Cairo financial support for this venture by arranging the sale of firearms. There was no commodity that

Abyssinians, from the highest to the lowest, desired more. Bell was determined on this second occasion to seek safety in numbers and travel with a larger party. Mansfield Parkyns, who was young and strong and as careless as Bell himself, seemed an ideal recruit, especially as he was discovered to be well armed and an excellent shot. Parkyns was delighted with the plan. He was now assured of making a start across Africa with a man of experience.

Two other candidates for inclusion in the party were staying at the hotel. They were Samuel Bevan who was employed as a courier to escort passengers between Alexandria and Suez on the overland route, and Walter Plowden, who had arrived from India, a country to which his family had provided officers and officials for years. Plowden was returning to England after giving up a commercial post in mysterious circumstances. Sam Bevan described him as a very agreeable companion who, hearing Bell talk about going to the source of the White Nile, 'could not rest until he had been received into the expedition as a volunteer, and being a fine well-built man, capable of great fatigue, and a good horseman withal, he promised to be an acquisition to the party'.

It was all rather informal considering the party's ambitious aims. It was apparent that an expedition led by Bell would travel light and require the minimum of preparation. Nor was there any cause to delay the departure of Bell, Bevan and Plowden. Parkyns, however, did not wish to start until the arrival of the equipment he had ordered from London. In any case, he had promised to accompany Milnes on an antiquarian tour of Upper Egypt. He therefore arranged with John Bell that he would join him in Abyssinia as soon as possible after returning from his tour with Milnes. He contrived to make it sound almost like a weekend expedition in the Home Counties, but Egyptologist Sir Gardiner Wilkinson reveals in his recently published Murray's Guide that even their proposed river trip may have had its grimmer side; he advises:

> The first thing to do after taking over the ship, is to sail it across the river and sink it. This will get rid of the rats and other noxious inhabitants it may have. However this must be done on the opposite shore and the ship must sail before night. Otherwise the rats will resume their berths on board.

Whether or not Richard Milnes saw fit to implement this precaution, his other arrangements for the river voyage to Upper Egypt were made with the generosity and competence to be expected of him. He took all the recommended equipment and creature comforts and was supported by a crew and a staff of servants that included his German valet, as well as a Maltese dragoman and a cook who carried some three hundred testimonials to his skill. What Milnes himself looked like after he had added dark spectacles to his 'Herculaneum mask' of a face, and surmounted it with a turban, one hesitates to imagine.

The party left Cairo for Upper Egypt in a fifty-foot river sailing-ship with two lateen sails. The cabin Milnes and Parkyns were to share in the stern Milnes thought to be not unlike 'one of the boxes at Vauxhall Gardens'. Their vessel was called *Zuleika*, whom Milnes, from his studies of Sale's Koran, now identified as Potiphar's wife, as well as Byron's heroine. Altogether, the trip had, from Milnes' point of view, a pronounced literary flavour, for it provided an amplitude of time – two months in fact – in which he could work on the verses that were eventually published as *Palm Leaves*. In it he described the voyage as:

> *Time that full at once could seem*
> *Of busiest travel and of softest rest.*

In his commonplace book, Milnes noted: 'The voyage up the Nile is agreeable anyhow, with good company most agreeable, and with objects of higher affection enchanting'. Before leaving England, he had proposed marriage to Florence Nightingale on more than one occasion, without success, after denying himself the attractions of one of the daughters of the Irish poet, Vere de Vere. He recommended Parkyns to turn Catholic and marry her.

Day after day they moved further south, sometimes sailing against the river current before the cool north wind, sometimes rowed or hauled by their apparently tireless watermen. Milnes and Parkyns lounged on the cushions in the cabin, surrounded by books, guns and maps, the awning making twilight of the blazing sun. It was a progress through the desert that underlined the advantages of having plenty of money with which to add amenity to the convenience of travelling by water. They passed an ever-changing scene of flat cultivations and groves of date palms, desert cliffs, villages, mosques, dovecotes, domed tombs, temples and pyramids. For Parkyns, there were sandgrouse, quail and red-legged partridge, white pelicans and purple Nile geese, herons and ibis, flocks of turtle doves and swallows, hoopoes and bulbuls, eagles, hawks, kites and vultures, to mention a few. Also, there were strange-looking fish, but only rumours of crocodiles, jackals and hyenas. Eliot Warburton, who was no naturalist, invited his readers to 'imagine everything disgusting and ingeniously horrid and monstrous, that can crawl, creep, buzz, or bite; imagine them in every place where they are most unwelcome, and most nauseous, and you will form some idea of the entomology of Egypt'. It delighted Parkyns.

Milnes found plenty of material for his commonplace book. It was his custom to fill a volume a year with the reflections of his 'magpie mind' : events, comments on events, anecdotes, biographical sketches, extracts from books he was reading. The volume for 1843 is embellished by some of Parkyns' illustrations, identifiable by the style of his drawing and the handwriting that goes with them, a beautifully formed script compared with Milnes' untidy scrawl. At the beginning of the volume he took two pages to illustrate in colour all the burgees of the different Nile vessels chartered by English tourists, together with the names of the vessels that wore them for purposes of recognition – *Bombay*, *Pyramid*, *Mummy*, *Backsheesh*, etc. Other illustrations by Parkyns are commendable sketches of the Hellenistic capitals at Kardessah and the like.

Elsewhere in his commonplace book, Milnes jotted down references to what John Bell said about Abyssinia as well as miscellaneous remarks by Parkyns. For example, 'Parkyns' principal interest in Lord Byron is because he was a Nottinghamshire man'; or 'Parkyns attributing the solidity and grandeur of old Egyptian architecture entirely to their love and consumption of *Beer*, as mentioned by Herodotus'; or, 'Parkyns says his sole ambition in life is that, behind his back and after his death, the poor should call him "good Mr. Parkyns".' They did, but there is no indication that at the time he recorded it, Milnes thought the remark to be less facetious than the others. Parkyns found the holiday an enervating experience, for Milnes noted that 'he seems to consider that nature had appointed two periods for repose – the night and the day'. It was not a state of indolence Parkyns could sustain indefinitely.

Milnes had brought a number of books with him and these were of direct educative value to both men. One of the merits of this lazy holiday was that it gave them time to read about matters that had begun to interest Milnes, apart from Egyptology and the history of Abyssinia.

A book he found particularly interesting was David Urquhart's *Spirit of the East*. Indeed, he declared that every visitor to the East should read it. One doubts whether many of them did because a critic described it, not unjustly, as 'wearily discursive and desultory'. Urquhart's political activities discredited him later in his career, but his explanation that all Ottoman subjects were not necessarily villainous heathens needed disseminating in English, even if it were only available to those who read his books.

A passage from *The Spirit of the East* that attracted Milnes' attention read:

> The man who sees the East should look with sympathy and interest on those institutions which live alone in the clime of the East . . . We naturally infer that good roads, mechanical skills, etc. are conditions of well-being, and, where these are not, everything must be degradation and misery.

Urquhart went on to give his readers examples of some of the differences between the attitudes and customs of Europe and those of the Ottoman Islamic realm and to demonstrate their triviality. They had a special attraction for Milnes, who was known to some of his contemporaries as the 'bird of paradox'. He noticed, as examples of such differences, that among the Turks a beard is a mark of dignity, but with Europeans of neglect; shaving of the head is, with Turks, a custom, with Europeans a punishment; in Turkey there were gradations of social rank without privileges, in Europe privileges without corresponding social distinctions; Turkish children had the manners of men, British men the manners of children; in the East, commotion may exist without disaffection, in Europe disaffection without commotion; Europeans termed the Turks pompous and sullen, the Turks called Europeans flippant and vulgar. One of Milnes' conclusions from his study of *The Spirit of the East* was that: 'a knowledge of the East involves long and assiduous application, which cannot be undertaken except by one who has no other occupation and is prepared to make an entire sacrifice of his accustomed comforts, luxuries and enjoyments'.

Milnes himself had no intention of experiencing the inconvenience of abnegation, but he may have suspected that Mansfield Parkyns would meet Urquhart's requirements. His young friend had time to spare and was too easy-going to have much compunction about sacrificing the comforts and luxuries to which he was accustomed. Moreover, it must have been apparent to Milnes that Parkyns had an unusual gift not only for making friends with all sorts of people but, more important, for enjoying the experience. Parkyns wrote:

> There is no difficulty in making agreeable acquaintance among the Arabs if one has but the humility to treat Orientals as friends . . . While up the Nile . . . instead of having, like most other travellers, to complain of the incivility of the sailors . . . they used to dispute among themselves which should accompany me on my excursions to carry my sketchbooks etc.

One can well believe it. They must have had a lot of fun with him.

In Egypt, Milnes was confronted with the overriding difficulty that he did not speak Turkish or Arabic, and very few Egyptians he regarded as his intellectual counterparts spoke a European language. Even if he had spoken Arabic one wonders what Milnes would have made of a discussion with a Muslim counterpart. Presumably a candidate might have been found among graduates from El Azhar mosque, the Muslim university in Cairo, who spent years studying the text of the Koran, Koranic exegesis, Islamic jurisprudence, theology, mysticism, logic, prosody and rhetoric, to name the main subjects. It was a more comprehensive curriculum, and a more exciting one than Cambridge offered in Milnes' day. But it lacked one all-important element from Milnes' point of view. It excluded speculation and inquiry. Being founded on belief in the divine inspiration of the Koran, 'innovation' had no place in Islamic education, indeed it was regarded as a cardinal error. It is unlikely that Milnes and his Muslim counterpart would have found common ground, or that there would have been a meeting of minds.

[26]

On the other hand, Mansfield Parkyns' attitude was in the tradition of those who do not feel equal to understanding other people's minds, but who have a sharp eye for their friendliness or hostility. Since it was in Parkyns' interests to make friends, his first step was to learn as much of the local language as he could.

Knowledge of a language and fluency in it, is an end in itself only for philologists. Count von Moltke, who had been adviser to the Turkish general defeated by Muhammed Ali Pasha in 1839, was reputed to speak seven languages and to be silent in all of them. Parkyns too would have been reduced to silence if he had been asked to discourse, even in English, on theology or prosody. In Arabic, Turkish or Tigrinya he was glad to talk ungrammatically to simple people about simple things of mutual interest, using a simple vocabulary, and to display that he enjoyed the conversation. He soon discovered that, especially among illiterate people, casual and untutored conversation is art and entertainment. Having tuned his ear and loosened his tongue, it was not too difficult a step to achieving friendly relations with people of different stations in life. He was able to convey his innate friendliness across a considerable cultural gap.

The *Zuleika* continued to the south, past Thebes, Edfu and Assuan, until Parkyns began to think that they might as well go the whole way to the Sudan. There was an argument reflected in one of Milnes' verses in *Palm Leaves*:

> *When you have lain for weeks together*
> *On such a noble river's breast . . .*
> *'Tis hard at some appointed place*
> *To check your course and turn your prow*

Milnes had his way, and they went about for Cairo. Not surprisingly, Parkyns found this preoccupation with verse more than he could stand. So he tried his hand at a parody:

> *All day drifted down,*
> > *Wind quite contrary;*
> *Dined in my dressing-gown*
> > *And sculled when it was airy;*
> *Smoked a new pipe-stick,*
> > *Which almost made me sick.*

[27]

The holiday had been a curious preliminary to travel in little-known parts of Africa, but it was what Parkyns needed. It may not have added much to his knowledge of what lay before him, but it had at least given him some idea of the immense distances involved, and also a glimpse of the desert itself. The Nile, for tourists, was the setting for ancient Egyptian remains; for geographers, a thread-like oasis across an immense desert; for Egypt, it was not only the source of their subsistence but also the way to the Sudan from which Egypt's rulers still hoped to derive wealth, and recruits for their armies. For Parkyns it was an invitation to exploration. The comfortable voyage gave Parkyns time to read something about the countries he was to visit, and to relate what he read to the stories he heard in Cairo. Moreover, his association with Milnes and his 'magpie mind' had introduced him to ideas and theories that other European explorers of Africa in the 19th century would have done well to ponder. Very few of them would have thought of learning from David Urquhart, or of relating his ideas to Africa.

3

The sail with the current back to Cairo did not take long; the quicker the better from Parkyns' point of view, for he was impatient to be off to the Red Sea and Abyssinia. Almost immediately Milnes left for London and more political disappointments. He next saw Cairo twenty-five years later when he came – as Lord Houghton – to represent the Royal Geographical Society at the opening of the Suez Canal, after the main geographical mysteries of Africa had been revealed. Milnes and Parkyns did not meet again for six years, but they exchanged letters as best they could between remote African addresses and Pall Mall.

It remained for Parkyns to complete his arrangements before he was on his way. Bell and Plowden had left while he was with Milnes on the Nile, but Sam Bevan, who had withdrawn from the Abyssinian party on the grounds that he was suffering from rheumatism, helped him to find the packing-case of equipment that had been mislaid in one of the transit company's warehouses. Unfortunately, some of the navigational instruments it contained had been irreparably damaged, preventing him from making the 'scientific observations' that were the hallmark of a serious explorer; a handicap that did not cause him concern at the time.

At Hill's hotel, Parkyns renewed his acquaintance with the pundits in Raven's snuggery and the vast Dr Abbott gave him a half-bred English whippet which accompanied him throughout his forthcoming travels. There is nothing so companionable to a traveller during long hours on foot, mule or camel as a dog trotting along, chasing small animals, baying to the moon at night, barking at everything that moves by day, and, in Africa, capable of running on two legs on the same side until the thorns in the paws on the other side have been removed.

Also, on Dr Abbott's recommendation, he engaged a Sudanese servant called Sa'id who had come to Cairo with the French staff officers Ferret and Galinier when they returned from Abyssinia in the previous year. Until he found his feet an experienced servant would be of importance to him, and Parkyns was fortunate in finding Sa'id. He had been purchased in the Sudan by Dr Rüppell in 1833 for 14 dollars and he came from one of the negroid tribes of Nuba in southern Kordofan that provided a steady supply of slaves to the market. With Rüppell in the Sudan and Abyssinia, and then with the French officers in Abyssinia, Sa'id had learnt how to prepare ornithological specimens for preserving and his skills were of considerable help to Parkyns. He paid him a wage twice that he had received from his French employers. Sa'id spoke Arabic of a kind – good enough for Parkyns to make a start on the language. In addition, he could make himself understood in Tigrinya, Amharic, French and German, and he was a fair cook. As for his appearance, his skin was so dark – the colour the Arabs call 'blue' – that on one occasion in Abyssinia, he was prevented by villagers from crossing the stream that supplied their drinking water, because they thought that he might turn it into ink. Although he must have known him intimately, for they shared several years of travel together, Parkyns did not have much to say about Sa'id except that his taste for strong drink was a problem and finally the cause of his death. It appears that Sa'id was not very bright and was inclined to lose his head in a crisis, although Parkyns appreciated his loyalty and willingness.

Since travelling with John Bell meant travelling light, Parkyns discarded many of his possessions, particularly the greater part of his English clothes and, in doing so, he confessed to a pang of nostalgia. While going through his things, he came across a package that reminded him of the life he was leaving and to which he might never return. The package contained the withered remains of the flowery buttonhole he had worn on his first appearance in what he described as 'the glorious, manly, picturesque costume of a swallow-tailed dress-coat'. Subsequently, when he found that the wearing of amulets was *de rigueur* in Abyssinia, he had the withered flowers stitched by a saddler into an amulet of his own which he hung round his neck and to which he attached superstitious significance. It was a charm that served him well until he lost it in circumstances that marked the end of a run of good luck.

Personal anecdotes of this kind mark another turning point in Parkyns' career as he prepared to leave Cairo. He began to keep a journal and we are able for the first time to learn from the evidence of his own pen what he was like at the age of twenty and how he reacted to the incidents of the journey he was undertaking.

Most of the original journal was lost in an accident some two years later, but Parkyns rewrote it soon afterwards, partly from memory, partly from some pages of the original that had survived, and partly from some notes that he was carrying separately. The surviving passages that were copied verbatim were those dealing with the earliest part of the journey; that is to say, his departure from Cairo and his voyage down the Red Sea. These are a periodical record by dates, although entries were not made daily. The parts of the journal written from notes made separately and from memory are grouped into subjects, although they keep roughly in sequence according to the occasions on which the different subjects attracted his attention.

The most interesting features of the journal, apart from the subject matter, are the high standard and consistency of Parkyns' handwriting despite the difficult conditions under which he wrote; the evidence that it provides of his efforts to learn literary Arabic; and the easy fluency of his English. The journal, as he explained in a preface, was not written with a view to subsequent publication, unlike the journals and diaries of so many travellers. It was a private account for his family and he was under no illusions about the unlikeliness of their ever seeing it, but the journal did eventually pass into the custody of his family and they have observed his wishes by keeping it in their possession. Nevertheless, most of its contents have been published because they formed the basis of the book, *Life in*

Abyssinia, which he was persuaded to write ten years later. It was published in two volumes by John Murray in 1853.

Parkyns had his own opinion about travellers' journals. He wrote:

> I hate journals in general; one gets so sick of reading dates, and at every ten lines meeting with the words 'Started at such a time'. Still, in some journeys, sea voyages, etc., there are no means of doing otherwise. With this apology, therefore, I begin, hoping that further on, as I reach more interesting scenes, my description of them will improve in proportion.

Nor had he much use for the portentous style usually adopted by African travellers, although he was in no danger of conforming to it. He was a much better writer than he imagined. Without compromising his individual responses to his experiences, he showed a notable ability for objective descriptions of the people he met: their appearance, clothes, food, habitations, customs generally and idiosyncrasies so far as he could identify them.

Early in March 1843, having heard from Suez that a dhow was leaving shortly for Jedda, he left helter-skelter. 'I left the inn mounted on a jack-ass (the cab of Cairo),' he wrote. He and Sa'id were soon through the Gate of Victory – that scene of return from so many disasters – after giving the password to the Albanian guards for the gates to be opened. Outside the walls:

> the fresh desert air blew on our faces . . . and had I been a poet I should no doubt have managed a neat poem of several cantos; or had I been a 'tourist', three pages of very feeling matter; but, being neither, I filled my pipe afresh and changed my donkey for a dromedary that was waiting for me.

It was now dark and, on his trotting-camel he went ahead with only Sa'id and a camel-driver, while the walking baggage-camel followed. At last he was on his own, with no other Englishman to tell him what to do, or how to behave.

In 1843, on average, only eight European passengers a week each way were using the Suez road, mostly in Mr Raven's vehicles. Yet each small steamship needed 3,000 camels to move its baggage, cargo and fuel; a requirement that brought temporary prosperity to the miserably poor camel-owning tribes of the area that had been deprived of their traditional subsistence from brigandage by Muhammed Ali Pasha. **Fifteen** years later, the construction of the railway from Cairo to Suez took the work from them. Signs of modernism and Western intrusion along the track were to be seen in the pieces of coal dropped from camel-loads of the fuel consigned to the steamships bunkering at Suez – one a fortnight. Hitherto, the usual fuel of the desert had been the droppings of camels rather than Welsh coal. Moreover, rest-houses, or stations, had been opened between Cairo and Suez in anticipation of increased traffic as a result of the introduction of the larger steamships by the P & O Steam Navigation Company.

When Parkyns reached No. 6 Station, far ahead of his baggage, he found that the manageress was 'a blooming young Englishwoman . . . She was really pretty, and apparently of respectable origin, for she played the piano'. She had married an Egyptian Copt who had been sent to England to learn shipbuilding, but she had not found married life with him in Egypt to her liking. Parkyns recorded in his journal that, having sent the baggage-camel ahead, he stopped to dine with the English manageress. Afterwards he

> started off at a fast trot which, after my dinner and several (I am afraid to say how many) bottles of porter etc., produced in me a violent pain in the bowels, which my servant assured all the world was the effect of poison administered to me by my late hostess whom he declared was in love with me and being anxious to retard my progress had administered the medicine . . . I never laughed more heartily or painfully in my life.

Parkyns arrived at Suez only to find that the dhow he had hurried to catch was not to leave for another week. 'So here I am stuck for a time in perhaps the most uninteresting place in the world; the town, if I may say so, ugly and the environs pure sand.' He found a congenial young officer from the Indian Army stranded there too.

> His company and a few excursions that I made, a little relieved the weariness of the stay . . . I went to see the place where Moses and the Israelites crossed, but though my philosophical companions saw something very interesting, I could see nothing but sand and sea.

[33]

Nearly three weeks passed until, on 25 March, both the delayed P & O steamer *Hindostan* arrived, and Parkyns' dhow sailed. The dhow was crowded: 'Arabs, blacks, Egyptians, Turks, Albanians, a durweesh Saint who wears a vast quantity of rags of various colours, and a lot of women; everyone doing his utmost to make as much noise as possible'. Having paid rather more than the others for his passage he was allowed to choose his place on board. A promising one seemed to be among part of the cargo under the poop:

> I scraped out a hole in the bags and other baggage and having made a quadrangle . . . I covered the whole with an old blanket. Such was my cabin and it was in no ways uncomfortable, although rather low, (average height about 2 feet by 9¾ inches).

It was tedious sailing. The dhows of the Red Sea were serviceable enough, and they often undertook voyages that belied their apparent limitations, but the ships showed little advance in design over the centuries, and their captains, who were not lacking in skill and courage, preferred to hug the treacherous coast, whenever possible, rather than venture into a better use of sea-space. Consequently, most European passengers, usually with experience of sea voyages, concluded, on insufficient grounds, that good seamanship and the Muslim fatalism of the dhow captains were incompatible. Some, particularly the British, could not resist the temptation to interfere. When James Bruce, the explorer of the Blue Nile, was sailing to a place he wished to visit in the Red Sea in the previous century, his small vessel was hit by a squall and he feared that it would be dismasted if the *rais* (captain) did not lower the sail. But the *rais*

> began apparently to lose his understanding with fright. I begged him to be steady . . . He answered me nothing, but that *Mahomet was the prophet of God* – Let him prophesy, said I, as long as he pleases, but what I order you is to keep steady to the helm and steer straight before the wind, for I am resolved to cut the main-sail to pieces, and prevent the mast from going away. I got no answer to this that I could hear, except something about the mercy and the merit of Sidi Ali Genowi . . . 'D—n Sidi Ali Genowi, said I, cannot you give me a

rational answer? Stand to your helm, or I will shoot you dead . . .' He answered only, Maloom, i.e., very well.

Parkyns was less interfering and concentrated on getting as much entertainment and instruction as he could from his fellow passengers. On one occasion, the dhow caught fire and he had the distracting experience of sitting on his powder-keg – '36 lbs of Harvey and Darton's superfine' – until the fire was extinguished amidst the admonitions of the men and the wails of the women.

At one of the coastal stops, Parkyns wrote that he:

went off in the morning and made a sketch of the neighbouring mountains etc. The scenery in the distance very wild and beautiful . . . bathed on the shore and returned in the evening. The people on board are now all my friends . . . they laugh and joke with me. One young man especially is my most intimate friend. He and another young man called Hassan . . . come every day to me to chat or learn a little one from another of our respective languages . . . I mentioned to him (Hassan) that I had always thought the life of a Beddow (nomad) a very pleasant one and that if I was not otherwise engaged I should have liked to have gone with him and settled for some time among his tribe.

Sailing in a dhow on the Red Sea was certainly different from drifting on the Nile in the well-found *Zuleika*, but Parkyns found his Arab acquaintances entertaining. Struggling to learn a new language, discovering the aesthetic resources of Arabic, and relating the language to the people and places about him all gave satisfaction to his inquisitiveness. Already he was trying to write in Arabic and he expressed regret at his lack of geological knowledge to enlighten him on problems presented to his eye by the scenery. Using his brain was a distraction he needed.

On arrival at Jedda, he was hospitably received by Mr Ogilvy, the British Vice-Consul, to whom he carried a letter of introduction from Richard Monckton Milnes. Ogilvy had been Milnes' contemporary at Trinity College, Cambridge, until he was sent down; an experience that may have given him a fellow-feeling for Parkyns. The latter, under the impression that Ogilvy's frequent intoxication was due to the loneliness of his life at Jedda, wrote to Milnes to ask if he could arrange for his transfer to a more congenial place.

Like other towns, Jedda was not to Parkyns' taste. Mosquito bites on his legs festered with sores (known locally as 'the Yemen plague') which he made worse by treating them with acetate of lead on the advice of an American who said he was a doctor. Parkyns' busied himself by writing letters before separating from a regular postal service. One of them was addressed to his former tutor telling him of his intention of going in search of the sources of the White Nile and, if possible, of crossing Africa, information that was communicated to the press in England. To Milnes, he wrote on 8 May 1843 complaining of his slow progress:

> You see where I am, and have been for twenty days by the date. I was 21 days at Suez (damn it!); 23 days on the Red Sea (damn damn it!!); and here 20 days (damn damn damn it!!!). But I go tomorrow.

His dhow sailed faster than the one from Suez, and was calling at Suakin, the port for the Sudan trade, and Massawa, the port for Abyssinia, as part of a voyage with the prevailing seasonal wind that would terminate in India. Massawa was Parkyns' destination. Of the ocean-going dhow, he wrote in his journal:

> in rough weather, she answers all the purposes of a patent bathing machine; her great safety consists in her bottom being like Paddy's shoes, full of holes, by which as fast as the water gets in, it runs out again. I have half of the cabin which is under the poop, the other half being occupied by a Turk's Hareem. Cockroaches are in swarms. I put my mouth last night to my waterbag to drink and was immediately covered from head to foot with these disgusting insects; everything is full of them, food and all. So at least after having probably eaten a dozen or 2 by mistake, I am now nearly accustomed to them.

After five days sailing, the apparently interminable line of hills on the African side, rugged against the setting sun, came into sight. While the ship dipped to the swell, its passengers drenched with moisture in the heat. Like Massawa, Suakin was within the jurisdiction of the Turkish *wali* (the governor) at

Jedda, although its inland trade was with the eastern Sudan, by conquest part of the Turkish province of Egypt. It was reached through a channel in the coral reef leading into a bay. In it the islet on which the town was built sits like a ball in a cup. From water-level, as Parkyns saw it, the place comprised some coral-stone houses, the white minarets of a few mosques and a collection of straw huts. The substantial buildings in the Arabian style that were to become a feature of the place had not yet been built. On the mainland behind were more habitations beyond which a flat plain spread itself towards the hills. At first sight the scenery, optically unstable in the heat, seemed to contain some vegetation, but this was an illusion: 'the vegetation,' Parkyns observed, 'consists of one solitary date tree in the village and a few dozen bushes'. The goats, camels and firewood collectors had removed the rest.

At once, Parkyns was asked to visit another Frank who was lying ill in a dhow that was due to sail for Jedda on the following day. He paddled over in a canoe to see him. It was Vignaud – Parkyns called him Vignon – a Frenchman who was one of the scientists with the French expedition to Abyssinia led by Lieutenant Lefebvre. Already he had lost three of his companions by disease or accident. Parkyns did what he could for Vignon, who had been geologist and draughtsman to the Lefebvre expedition, and sat up with him all night. But he was too far gone and looking after him was a disturbing experience. 'Poor Vignon!' Parkyns wrote:

I heard of his death at Jeddah shortly after my arrival at Massawa. When his vessel left us I could almost have mourned him as an old friend, though I had seen so little of him . . . I reflected that such would probably be my end also, sooner or later, such being the lot of most of those whom science, curiosity, or a wandering taste lures under the fatal branches of that most deadly of upas-trees, 'African discovery'.

In spite of his ineffectual attentions to the Frenchman, Parkyns' fellow-passengers now credited him with special medical skills in addition to those usually suspected to be latent in educated Europeans. People with all kinds of diseases sought his help, including a local tribesman with a knife wound that ran the width of his shoulders, for which the patient asked

Parkyns 'for a plaster'. In addition to local patients, many of the passengers of his dhow were ill, and the ulcers on his own legs were worse, so bad that he could not go ashore. In his journal he commented: '*Sic mare, sic terrens* might almost be said in truth in these latitudes; on land, on sea, all are sick'.

While Parkyns was sailing past the flat Dahlak Islands outside Massawa where, it was said, the pearls that adorned the crowns of both the pharaohs of Egypt and the doges of Venice had grown, he had his first sight of Ras Ghedem. It is a shapely mountain – a landmark – at the southern end of a wide bay of which Massawa island forms the northern extremity. Massawa itself looked exactly what it was – another small Turkish outpost with its cluster of single-storied houses, mostly of wood and straw, a stone one for the 'governor', one or two mosques and domed tombs and not a tree or bush to vary the scene. Behind, against the setting sun, were the mountains, closer to the sea here, and higher – up to eight thousand feet and often obscured by cloud and the heat-haze. They were not only a promise of *terra firma* but also of cool mountain air; to a European the most desirable alternative to the hot salty misery of the sea and the coast. Parkyns wondered whether Bell and Plowden had yet reached the plateau. At Jedda, a dhow captain had told him that they had not yet reached Massawa when he had visited the port not long before, and Consul Ogilvy had said that the two men did not seem to be getting on well together.

Parkyns' impatience to leave the dhow is understandable: 'I tumbled into a boat and got ashore immediately'. After what he had heard in Cairo about the number of Europeans visiting Massawa, it was no surprise to find a white man of unusual appearance standing on the shore asking whether there were any letters for him from Jedda. He turned out to be a man Parkyns had heard of from Mr Ogilvy as the person who would be able to supply his needs when he reached Massawa: Angelo Bracha, the Jewish merchant from the Levant who came to Massawa as dragoman to the French expedition led by Lieutenant Lefebvre in 1839. When Parkyns met him, he was acting for M. Degoutin, the French vice-consul. He spoke Italian to Parkyns and he informed him that Bell and Plowden had passed through Massawa some weeks earlier. By now, they should be established in Adwa.

Parkyns' first requirement was for accommodation because he needed a safe place in which to deposit his arms, equipment and presents. So Angelo took him to the compound used by the French vice-consulate which was now in Angelo's care. Then, being wise in the ways of Turkish officials, Angelo took him without delay to pay his respects to the Turkish *kaimakam*. He was shown into what appeared to be a shed which he thought to be

> one of the most miserable huts that human invention could possibly make of sticks and straws·. . . His Excellency seemed not to take the slightest attention beyond desiring me to be seated, which I did among a crowd of sailors, beggars, etc. . . . The fact is, my costume was not of the most elegant; and, as in all countries men are judged by either their dress or their company, it was not likely that Rustum would form a very high opinion of me, appearing as I did.

He might have recalled David Urquhart's dictum, 'that a European's dignity is lost when he get beyond the influence of laundresses and shoe blacks'. Wisely he decided not to throw his weight about but rather, as far as possible, to go unnoticed.

After a couple of days temporary accommodation in the French compound, Angelo found Parkyns another place that contained a stone storeroom for his gear, and a grass shed, open to the wind and looking out over the sea, for his own accommodation.

> The bed is aloft like the berth in a steamer, with a little entrance like the door of a pigeon house . . . In the evening I can get a nice sea breeze and watch the pretty Galla girls of a neighbour as they wash themselves.

At other times he walked to Angelo's shop where he spent his time gossiping in Italian and studying, unconsciously, *homo sapiens* in forms quite new to him. This was the kind of occupation that an explorer with an eye on the medals of learned societies, and newspaper headlines, would leave himself insufficient time to enjoy. In any case one imagines that some of them would have thought Angelo – described by Parkyns as 'the oddest-looking fish I ever had seen out of water' – to be unsuitable company.

Parkyns thought differently. 'My friend Angelo', he wrote:

[39]

made himself very agreeable during my stay. He was a perfect oddity of his kind – a great boaster, and consequently a little doer . . . I have frequently sat in his shop, thinking of the past and planning for the future, while the worthy little man was handing out farthingsworth of pepper and ha'p'orths of sugar.

As for the people of Massawa, he observed that they

'are, as would be naturally expected, in such a climate, rather weak, and wanting in energy. Their subsistence is derived entirely from commerce, – a line of life particularly suitable, as affording them means of using the mind, while at the same time, the body is enjoying 'otium cum dignitate', stretched out on the benches of a cafe. I have heard many Europeans speak of the severe effect the heat had on them. Strange to say, during the short time I passed at Massawa, I never suffered at all. The whole day was spent by me in running about, either catching insects in the sun, or otherwise actively employing myself.

Angelo was as well informed as any about the movements of European travellers in Abyssinia, since most of them had been his customers in one way or another since he left the service of Lieutenant Lefebvre. In the last five years, about two dozen Europeans, at a rough estimate, had passed through Massawa, and some had not returned. Parkyns was soon to learn that this number could easily be lost from view in a mountainous country with the poorest of communications. However, many of these travellers had written accounts of their experiences and nearly all mentioned the difficulties of travelling from Massawa to the highlands through valleys commanded by the Saho tribes. There was no great danger but the Saho could cause delay and the Turkish authorities at Massawa had long since decided that it was hopeless to try and keep order among them. Instead, they made an agreement with the headman of the village on the mainland opposite Massawa – Arkiko – to keep the peace in return for charging certain dues from those in transit and a subvention from the Turkish authorities. The headman was known as the *naib* or deputy. European travellers usually bargained with him over the amount they paid for protection during their journey to the highlands, but Parkyns left this to Angelo and sent Sa'id to Arkiko to pay the dues.

Having been assured by Angelo that Bell and Plowden would not go beyond Adwa before the end of the rains, Parkyns was no longer in a hurry to rejoin them. He said goodbye to Angelo, having judged correctly that, however much an oddity, he was a man who could be trusted to keep his word to a friend, and he left his remaining surplus possessions with him to be sent on later to Adwa with any letters that might arrive from Jedda. In the meantime, Parkyns wanted to visit the medicinal hot springs at Ailet, inland from Massawa at the foot of the main escarpment, to see if treatment there would benefit his ulcerated legs. In particular he wanted to confirm the accounts of previous travellers that there was exceptionally good shooting in these foothills. Elephant and lion were still to be found in the area apart from a tempting variety of other game and birds.

On the day of his departure, the camels Parkyns had hired did not appear at the time arranged. So he left Sa'id to look after his things while he crossed in a canoe to the mainland and went ahead on foot. Even the uninviting mainland environs of Massawa seemed exciting to him:

> The whole air was alive with insects of every variety both in species and hue, many of them most brilliantly coloured; and as I advanced farther inland, I observed two or three different varieties of sun-birds . . . Wandering on, I came to a place where the sea runs in like a creek, and I took the opportunity of refreshing myself and paying to the salt water my last visit for many years. The water was above five feet deep, with a smooth sand bottom. Nothing could be more delicious, – far preferable to the finest marble swimming-bath in Europe.

After his swim, he set out again and met the man with the camels he had hired, on his way to Massawa. Having been assured that he was on the right road, and having told the camel-driver to collect his servant and baggage and follow quickly, he continued on his way.

> Excited to the highest pitch by the workings of my fertile imagination, which induced me to expect every moment to tumble into a Happy Valley, I almost ran along, bearing such a load of castles in my head as would have puzzled

Hercules to carry, had they been constructed of any other material but air . . . Description cannot convey the feeling of one who for the first time feels himself really in a tropical country; the burning sun, the red sand, the bright green of the trees, the purple sky, the difference from England where all nature is moderated in its tone. Here all is in extreme; colour, heat and all.

The few local people he met – pastoral nomads – and the wildlife, all seemed to be in harmony.
Needless to say, he lost his way.

I proceeded some distance till I came to three roads all of which appeared to differ in tendency very little one from the other. I therefore like *Don Quichotte's Rossinante* took the first that came, and went on enjoying myself amazingly.

As it was getting dark, he came across some young slave-girls who were out collecting wood and they guided him to the village of Monsoulle from where Massawa gets its water. He found living there the wife of the French Consul, in the absence of her husband trying to escape the heat of the port. She invited him to spend the night in the compound of her straw house and regaled him with stories of the perils of travel in Abyssinia, but he was tired out and soon fell asleep.

4

The pattern of Mansfield Parkyns' experiences in Africa was determined by the travel arrangements he adopted when he left Massawa. If he had had European companions he would have spent much of his time talking to them in a European language at the expense of conversation with his African comrades. He preferred to be alone. If he had had a tent, he would have cut himself off from contact with his African companions and from those in whose houses he stayed. These were unconventional preferences that his British contemporaries found difficult to understand. Nor did he try to preserve the comforts that most Europeans regarded as basic. Indeed, he seems to have regarded physical civilization as a superfluous nuisance, and it never occurred to him that 'appearances' had anything to do with the impression he gave of himself, either to Europeans or Africans. For practical reasons, he decided on leaving Massawa that he must relieve himself of European encumbrances, so he left his baggage until he might have need of what remained of it:

> My best articles of European dress were offered to my friend Angelo, as recompense for his kindness . . . From the day I left Suez (March 25, 1843), till about the same time in the year 1849, I never wore any article of European dress, nor

indeed slept on a bed of any sort, – not even a mattress . . .
For more than three years (that is until I reached Khartoum)
I wore no covering to my head; nor to my feet, except the
horny sole which a few months' rough usage placed under
them.

As for food, he followed the precept that 'what does not
poison, fattens'. His belief in frugal living was fortunate, for, as
he explained:

The are no good cooks in Abyssinia, and the tap is of the
most inferior quality; but the semi-starvation to which one is
now and then reduced, so far from being a hardship in
travelling, as it is often represented by tourists, is, if not
continued to extremity, one of the greatest possible blessings.

Certainly it was a regime that suited Parkyns because
throughout his stay in Abyssinia his health seems to have been
remarkably good. This was partly due to his common sense in
not exposing himself to malaria by keeping to the highlands
and avoiding places where there was standing water. When he
was obliged to travel in places where malaria was endemic, he
slept between two large fires at night, when he could get the
firewood. In addition, he followed the local custom of covering
himself completely with 'his cloth', including his head, at night,
a further protection from mosquito bites. Even so, he was lucky
to avoid both malaria and amoebic dysentery.

Parkyns was also a believer in the beneficial effects of the
sun's rays:

It is customary to hold the sun in great dread. I do not
pretend to say whether my constitution in this respect differs
from that of other men; but, for my part, I never retired into
the shade to avoid the noonday heat; and I never wore any
covering to my head except the rather scanty allowance of
hair with which nature has supplied me, with the addition
occasionally of a little butter. During the whole of that time, I
never had a headache.

He considered that in India the evils attributed to exposure
to the sun should have been blamed on the consumption of too
much food and drink. This was medical heresy indeed.

His departure from Cairo had been informal enough, but

from Mme Degoutin's house at Monsoulle, he simply strolled off towards the foothills of the main escarpment where game and birds were said to be plentiful. It was an area with a good supply of water, grazing and deciduous trees resulting from the higher local humidity created by the contact between the warm air of the Red Sea and the steeply rising hills. The wild animals that once abounded there have disappeared since the railway and main road from Massawa to Asmara on the plateau above were constructed through the area, but Parkyns, before the sun was high, had already encountered guineafowl, partridge, several kinds of gazelle and a jackal in the dry watercourses of the arid coastal plain. He shot enough for the next meal. This was his first taste of African 'sport'.

To Englishmen of Parkyns' generation, a 'sportsman' meant one thing above all else: one who found enjoyment in open-air pursuits, usually at the expense of wildlife that seemed to abound in unlimited quantities. The killing of 'game' was the diversion, and sometimes the entire concern, of the English gentry. Today, to most people, it seems to have been an unfortunate aberration. Then, no one doubted that birds had been created to be shot on the wing, and foxes to be killed by hounds.

Of course, 'sportsmen' went far beyond shooting for the pot, or for providing zoological specimens. Consequently, Parkyns' views on sportsmanship created misgivings among his contemporaries. For example, a reviewer of his book, *Life in Abyssinia*, when it appeared ten years later in 1853 concluded that:

> there is something in the author's description of wild animals and the mode of taking them that makes us doubt whether he is a sportsman at heart. A good companion doubtless, a staunch comrade in the wilderness, but still we cannot help fancying *no sportsman*.

The reviewer's concern was understandable in view of Parkyns' attitude. He explained:

> I cannot help saying that it appears to me the height of folly and wanton cruelty to slaughter some fifty brace of inoffensive birds for the mere sake of boasting of it as a feat. No sport would ever induce me to kill more than was required for the kitchen.

[45]

His heresy went beyond this.

I never shoot flying, considering that unsportsmanlike. A true sportsman shows his skill by getting up to his game unperceived, when, putting the muzzle of his gun as close to the tail feathers as he possibly can, he blazes away into the thick of the covey. At any rate this is the only way you can shoot in a country where if you entirely expend your powder and shot you must starve, or else make more, as I have been obliged to do many a time. I cannot understand how people in Europe can enjoy shooting, where one is dependent on a crowd of keepers, beaters, dogs, sandwiches, grog, etc., walking up and down a turnip or cabbage garden, varied with a stubble field or a potato-bed! Fine sport, verily! Or you find a hare sitting quietly at your feet; so you administer a kick on her posteriors, and then shoot her when she attempts to escape, thereby adding injury to insult.

In Africa, it was considered that sportsmen should observe certain formalities verging on ritual. Parkyns ignored them:

My sole companion on ordinary occasions is the little boy who carries my rifle while I carry my gun, and we do all the work ourselves. His sharp eyes, better accustomed to the glare than my own, served me in every point as well as a setter's nose.

Parkyns spent three weeks in these foothills, shooting game and watching and collecting birds, sometimes visiting the medicinal springs at Ailet to soak his ulcerated legs. During this time he began to observe the life in village and encampment:

The people of Ailet are very sociably inclined. In the evening, parties of the men might be seen congregated about the doors of each other's houses to chat. Towards me they were particularly friendly.

Of course, when he went shooting, a dozen or more followed him because (although Parkyns did not realize it) he was in their eyes a heaven-sent supplier of the protein for which their emaciated bodies hungered. Even so, these Muslims would not eat unless the wounded animal's throat was cut in the ritual manner to the accompaniment of the phrase 'In the name of God: God is most great'. It was a sign that he was among

Christian Abyssinians when the phrase was changed to: 'In the name of the Father, the Son, and the Holy Ghost'. However he found that there was a dispensation when the animal was shot dead before its throat could be cut. In these circumstances 'they consider it sufficient to think the words while in the act of pulling the trigger'.

Perhaps it was the frugality of the Saho herdsmen in the valleys leading to the plateau above that impressed him most. In spite of long marches over rocky mountainous tracks, his lean companions could live on a diet that would be equated to starvation in Europe. He found that he too could live on it. The main meal, while he was with these nomads, consisted of some flour and water mixed into a stiff dough and kneaded into balls, 'each the size and form of a nine-pound shot'. A round stone was then heated in the fire and pushed into the ball of dough and the dough formed round it. The whole was put into the embers of the fire, turned round once or twice while baking for ten minutes, and then eaten. Parkyns thought that 'the only fault to find with bread thus made is, that seldom more than the outside and inside surfaces are at all baked'.

He was thoroughly enjoying himself when he was interrupted by the arrival of a messenger from Walter Plowden. Since the previous month, he and John Bell had been ill with malaria. They had advanced towards the highlands, but stopped at the village of Kiaquor (Parkyns' spelling), beyond which Plowden could go no further. Kiaquor is the first Christian village a traveller encounters on this track, which, in modern times, has become the main motor road from Massawa to the interior of Abyssinia.

Since Plowden showed no sign of improvement, Bell went ahead to Adwa to prepare accommodation, leaving Plowden to follow as soon as he was well enough to travel. Naturally, Parkyns lost no time in responding to Plowden's appeal to come to his assistance, although he was clearly disappointed at having to leave a place he enjoyed. So, with Plowden's messenger and a guide from a local tribe, he left the following morning. They carried only their bare necessities, including Parkyns' paintbox and a flask of rum, without donkeys or mules to help.

Access to the highlands from the coastal plain at this point is along valleys running at an angle to the edge of the plateau, which gradually gain height until they end in a steep ascent to

the crest. The valley Parkyns and his companions were following became deeper and the tangle of hills that flanked it became
a steep-sided mountain covered with thorn scrub that turned
into juniper on the summit. Above them was the ancient
monastery of Bizen and they had to climb to a height to cross
the saddle into the next valley. The going was rough:

> covered with large, round, loose stones, and well garnished
> with the usual proportion of thorny trees, neither of which, as
> may be imagined, contributed to the comfort of a bare-footed
> pedestrian. . . . I had up to this time so far retained old habits
> as to wear sandals; but even sandals proved inconvenient on
> exchanging the sandy plain for the stony hills; so, following
> the advice and example of my companions, I took them off
> and carried them in my hands. Before my feet got well
> hardened I suffered considerably, though not so much as I
> expected, for the use of sandals is a good preparation for
> going barefoot, as a great deal of sand gets between them and
> the foot.

It took two hours to reach the crest between the two valleys,
but Parkyns felt rewarded by the view, 'rough and wild in the
extreme'. Unfortunately his tired servant threw himself on the
ground and spilled one of their few luxuries, a drinking horn of
honey.

> Without stopping to speak, we all rushed forward, knocking
> our heads together from eagerness, and sucked up the little
> honey that the greedy sand had left on the surface. What
> can't be cured must be endured so washing out the honey-
> horn with about a quart of water, and adding thereto a
> tablespoon of rum, I presented my companions with a
> convivial bowl of punch . . . though it was nearly pure water.
> Imaginary enjoyment is a very agreeable thing in the abs-
> ence of the reality.

On the following day, the track seemed to become even worse
until they suspected that the guide was lost. Only the cooler
temperature and the flattening of the valley indicated that they
were making progress to the highlands. Then, just before
sunset, they came to a level patch in the hills and, as the light
was fading, they heard the lowing of cattle and saw the fires of
an encampment. The Saho nomads received the small party

hospitably with a large bowl of milk and some **hides to sleep on.**
Then on again the next morning along the Ala plain, an open
space between the hills, which can be seen to be on the last step
below the crest of the escarpment. Both climate and scenery
were changing and Parkyns found time to do two or three
sketches in water-colour.

Kiaquor and the ailing Plowden were not far off, and, by the
afternoon, the party was able to reach its destination, a village
surmounted by a Christian church on a hill, with the rocky
escarpment that marks the limit of the plateau beyond it. There
was no doubt about what to do with Plowden, whom Parkyns
found very weak and 'thoroughly sick of Kiaquor'. They agreed
to leave as soon as possible for Adwa, where John Bell should
have had time to become properly established. In fact they
started on the next day, a larger party now, for Plowden, whose
Indian experience had not taught him to employ Parkyns'
informal methods, had eight porters for his luggage and a spare
mule which Parkyns could ride. Off they moved towards the
boulder-strewn slopes, above which lay the Abyssinian
plateau.

On a mule, the ascent along a track that traversed the rocky
hillside was not a great problem, for the Abyssinian mule is the
surest-footed of load-carrying quadrupeds, and almost inex-
haustible. So it was only an hour or two before they reached the
top and could look back on the scene of mountain ranges and
valleys through which they had come, now full of white clouds
rising from the Red Sea. It was a scene that Parkyns, but not
Plowden, viewed for the last time. What they saw ahead soon
effaced their memory of it.

Looking inland from the crest, there were no higher hills in
the close vicinity, although some big ones could be seen in the
distance. It was a varied landscape that invited progress to see
what might lie beyond. No wonder that highland Abyssinians
arriving from the Red Sea plain broke into song as they came
over the crest of the escarpment, or that they threw a stone on to
the cairns that mark the places from which a Christian church
first comes into view. However, Parkyns soon became aware
that although the soil looked fertile enough, this southern part
of Hamasien province was no Happy Valley, for the villages
had been burnt down and the crops abandoned. 'Civil war,' he
wrote,

the perpetual scourge of Abyssinia, and the principal cause of its remaining in its present state of poverty and barbarism, had passed over this fair land, and reduced it to such a state that wherever you turned you saw nothing but devastation and ruin.

Although he did not know it, he was witnessing the beginning of what, in its modern form, became the 'Eritrean problem', a subject about which he would become better informed by those without first-hand knowledge of it.

After crossing through the great rocks on the north side of the Gura plain, and then across the upper reaches of the River Mareb, the party travelled in a southerly direction towards Adwa over fairly level uplands devoid of trees, and daily swept by torrential rainstorms. In due course they reached the edge of the plateau at a point where the cliffs fall towards the valley of the Mareb as it turns west; an emphatic geographical feature dividing the main part of Tigré from its northern extension, later to be given the title of Eritrea by the Italian invaders. The view across the valley to the great monolithic hills above Adwa is magnificent. After a slow day's march with the ailing Plowden, they forded the river waist-deep in the muddy water, with Plowden being carried across in a litter. Then there was a further two-day's-climb out of the valley towards Adwa, with the sugar-loaf mountains coming nearer by the hour.

Shortly after crossing the river, they were told by a passer-by that there were two Europeans encamped not far away, although it turned out to be another three hours before they reached their tent among the hills. Parkyns was welcomed cordially by Father de Jacobis, the leader of the Roman Catholic mission, and the German naturalist, Wilhelm Schimper. Parkyns found himself in the presence of a problem about which he had heard much during his journey; the contest between the Protestant and the Roman Catholic missionaries in Tigré. Moreover, it explained an experience he had had while travelling on the north side of the Mareb. During a stop at a village, he had taken a walk between showers, 'partly to procure us a supper, and partly to enjoy the scenery', and he noticed a party of travellers moving at a lower level and heading in the direction of Massawa. His attention was attracted by the presence among the party of a man who appeared to be a European. When he returned to the village, Parkyns inquired who the white man might be. He recorded:

Some of our people guessed him to be a Greek silversmith; others a Copt who was leaving the Abuna on his way to Egypt. But the most prevalent opinion was that he was an Anglo-German missionary who was returning to Europe having been roughly turned out of the country.

Father de Jacobis cleared up the mystery by telling him that the European was, in fact, Mr Isenberg, the German Protestant in the service of the Church Missionary Society of London. Isenberg had planned to by-pass Adwa and go direct to see the Abuna (the Patriarch of the Abyssinian Church) at Gondar, but his plan failed and he was ordered to the coast under escort.

The next experience in prospect for Parkyns would be his arrival at Adwa and, from all he had read and heard, he supposed that it was a place of some importance. To reach it from the north the traveller makes a steady climb from the Mareb until, having entered the hills, one notices that the valleys are falling to the south; towards the next large river, the Takazze, some sixty miles beyond Adwa. The scene that holds the attention on the approach to Adwa is that provided by the mountains to the left: huge trachytic monoliths rising to nearly four thousand feet above the plateau and ten thousand above sea level. Closer inspection shows that they are more widely dispersed in plan than they appear to be in the perspective of a rider on a mule. Fifty years after Parkyns first saw them, they were to provide the macabre setting for the battle in which the invading Italian army suffered its terrible defeat in 1896; a defeat that invited the revenge taken forty years later.

As Parkyns and Plowden approached Adwa, they saw before them a more conventional line of hills and, on the slope opposite them, the town. It had to be reached across a grassy meadow and over the stream that had cut into it. As they rode, the afternoon clouds darkened and the curtains of rain in the distance began to close in a deluge. Thunder reverberated through the streaming hills and lightning struck perpendicularly to the ground. 'I galloped on ahead of the party,' Parkyns recalled, 'anxious to obtain shelter as soon as possible.' His mule was tired and the ground muddy and slippery. Crossing the bed of the stream at the foot of the town was particularly awkward. He slid into it and had to clamber out on the other side 'to the extreme delight of some young gentlemen collected on the top who laughed and yelled at each successive mishap'.

The town was hardly what he had expected from his preconceived notions of Adwa. He knew, for example, that the market supported merchants on one of the trade routes of the country and that it was situated in the ancient Aksumite kingdom that had fallen a thousand years ago. Surely, in its buildings and urban facilities, Adwa would live up to something approaching its historical and commercial reputation? He was to be disappointed, for:

> the rain driving in my face, I could not, till within a short distance of it, see enough to enable me to determine whether Adoua was built in the Grecian or Moorish taste. I own I rather expected to see columns or obelisks, if not an acropolis on some of the neighbouring hills. Judge then of my astonishment when, . . . I found nothing but a large straggling village of huts, some flat-roofed, but mostly thatched with straw, and the walls of them built of rough stone, laid together with mud in the rudest possible manner!

5

John Bell had recovered from his bout of malaria and was established in a round stone house in the Salaamji quarter of Adwa, that is to say, in the small area on the hillside where the indigenous Muslim traders, or *jabarti*, and any visiting foreigners settled. It was not luxurious accommodation, but it kept out the rain and provided more reliable shelter than was usually obtainable. Above it on the hillside is the church of the Saviour of the World, a welcome sanctuary for many a hard-pressed unfortunate. Early in the morning, from under its wide conical roof behind tall trees, came the chanting, or wailing, of the numerous deacons of the church, which could be heard in the houses below. Sometimes one could hear the unmusical percussion of the flat stone that, when struck by a smaller stone, served as a bell, 'resembling', Parkyns commented:

> that of a small village church in Rutland, of which I remember having heard it said, that, when ringing for church, it had sometimes occurred to strangers visiting the place on a Sunday that the people were a very Sabbath-breaking set, as the blacksmith was working away as usual.

The appearance of Adwa was less alarming when the sun shone on it, and Parkyns was soon noting the special visual qualities of the highlands of Tigré. The journey up the deep valleys from the Red Sea, his emergence into the unexpected scenery beyond the escarpment, and its arid, sculptured horizons, the candelabra euphorbias and the variety of trees and birds in the hollows, the thin mountain air and burning sun, the changed perspective of the clouds, all contributed to the novelty.

The people as well as the scenery had a special character. The lean, wiry men with dark skins and reputations for dark deeds in battle had aquiline features and a brisk step. They were soon to be of more interest to him than the country's scenery and geography. Unlike most European visitors, Parkyns assumed that they had individuality, rather than being part of the conglomeration of defects in character and conduct that had repelled other travellers. The graceful and apparently untiring women had neatly tressed hair plaited closely to their skulls in the local fashion. They were to be seen carrying loads in the wake of their menfolk and yet chattering in lively, if plaintive tones. To Parkyns, all were individuals. Their modes of greeting, their mutual bowing and embracing, reminded him that he was in the presence of a civilized tradition. Christian institutions were evident in every village. There were churches in quiet groves of trees, and priests copying texts in the Ge'ez script after killing a goat and flaying its skin to provide the parchment. There was a general atmosphere of proximity to the Old Testament.

Parkyns had not yet learned much about the political structure of the country, but a common sight passing through the scenery was that of an impassive 'baron', one of the local placemen who had a feudal look about him and a dignity that reflected a sense of historical continuity, however undesirable. A couple of muskateers might come first, carrying their prestigious weapons with feathers in their muzzles. Then the placemen's horse, saddled and led before him, with the incumbent himself following on a mule under a straw sunshade, flicking the flies away with a whisk made of a horse's tail, or a giraffe's tail if he were senior enough; and behind him a drummer, or several drummers, to indicate his rank. Then, if he could support them, armed retainers with their shields, swords and spears, followed by women carrying horns of honey, or mead or other culinary necessities.

With the smattering of the local Tigrinya language acquired

during his previous visit, John Bell was a man to give confidence to Parkyns and Plowden. He had acquaintances among the merchants and he knew how to wear his Abyssinian clothes and how to conduct everyday relations with his neighbours and with Abyssinians generally without giving too much offence. Foreigners were known as Copts, or Christian Egyptians, and Parkyns found that they were believed to have two interests and skills: the coining of money and the ability to find forgotten hiding places of gold and treasure. In addition, they were expected to have plenty of presents awaiting distribution, as well as firearms for sale, and greatly-prized knowledge of how to repair damaged weapons. It all added up to their being regarded as figures of curiosity and envy.

Whenever they went out, the visitors were followed and importuned. It was only later that comments on his appearance, which Parkyns thought at the time to imply admiration, turned out, after he had learned some Tigrinya, to have been less than complimentary: 'such as "Cat's eyes", "Monkey's hair", "What nice red morocco their skin would make for a sword-sheath!" etc.'. After he was well-established in Tigré, he asked someone who had never previously seen a white man what his first impression of him had been: 'He answered me very simply that I resembled a rather good-looking Abyssinian who had lost his skin'.

After Parkyns had been at Adwa for a week or two, his servant Sa'id arrived from Massawa with several loads of his possessions, mostly supplies of powder and shot, presents and the like. Naturally, the eye of the *negad ras*, or merchants' chief, fell on them, and claims that he should examine them for the assessment of customs dues followed. The *negad ras* was a Muslim who paid the ruler of Tigré an annual sum for the privilege of collecting dues on merchandise passing through the town. Perhaps it was Parkyns' lack of appreciation for the commercial ethos that made him so resistant to suggestions that if he paid a certain sum, his baggage would not be examined for full payment of customs dues. He insisted that he had no merchandise but only things he needed for his trans-African journey, which would take years. One can well understand that the *negad ras* had difficulty in understanding this. However, since the baggage contained presents for the ruler of Tigré, Ras Oubie, Parkyns declared, on Bell's advice, that he

[55]

would put the matter to the ruler as soon as possible. In any case, a visit to the ruler's camp at Howzayn to deliver their presents could be delayed no longer.

Their journey to Howzayn was impeded by the daily rain that fell. Plowden was still having attacks of fever. Once when they halted, Parkyns himself suddenly fainted, presumably from starvation. They had deep valleys to cross with hard climbs out of them and at most stopping places they were not welcome because the villagers were tired of entertaining stragglers from the ruler's army at Howzayn. However, at one village they were given honey, milk and eggs because one of Parkyns' retainers had a relative living there.

Not so at the next, where they were mistaken for soldiers or robbers. Finally they settled in the house of an old woman who protested shrilly. Parkyns recalled:

> I felt pity for her as, remaining near the hut, she kept prowling about on some excuse or other . . . sobbing all the while in a most piteous manner. At last, feeling for the old creature, I gave her a little present, and taking her by the hand assured her that she had nothing to fear from us. This reassured her . . . and at night she brought in all her treasures, and lay down in a corner of the hut behind me, as if to put herself under my protection.

Perseverance brought them under the formidable cliffs of the Haramat mountain, a large example of a Tigrean *amba*, or flat-topped mountain, with precipitous sides that made it easily defensible. This one, they were told, had long been the refuge of a celebrated robber and the Abyssinians in the party hurried on, expressing their misgivings.

Tired out, they reached Howzayn to find a small town in a wide valley, with plenty of water and grazing for the animals. It was an excellent place for Ras Oubie to pitch his camp for the rains. Not being indigenous to Tigré, he had no family residence to attract him.

Arrival to the 'royal' camp, or rather the camp of the paramount chief of the period, was often the climax of a foreign visitor's expectations, but none of the three Englishmen who arrived at Howzayn in August 1843 anticipated staying in Tigré, and certainly their appearance at the camp created minimal interest. Europeans had been seen in Tigré for years and some recent visitors had attracted criticism.

As a result of John Bell's previous visit to the country, he was already acquainted with a functionary who had then been nominated as his *balderraba*, or 'introducer'. This was Bejur-undi Cafti, the steward of Ras Oubie's household, and it was to his dwelling that the visitors made their way. Unfortunately, he was absent on a punitive expedition, but his brother Negussi acted for him and volunteered to procure an audience with the ruler without delay. In the meantime, some disgruntled soldiers were turned out of their hut to make way for them, and the three Englishmen settled down in a space 'about seven feet in diameter, and five and a half high at the highest part'. There they waited; 'sitting on the carpet of patience, eating the bread of disappointment'.

It soon became clear that there would be no other bread for them unless they ceased to rely on the ruler's hospitality. They supposed that Negussi was starving them into giving him a better present than they intended. Finally, they were obliged to send a servant round the camp crying: 'Who has bread for money?' They had to pay eight times the usual price for the little that was forthcoming.

Yet all and sundry asked for presents. Among them was Ras Oubie's nine-year-old son who had to be given Parkyns' French cuirassier's sword which was nearly as long as himself. Then a man arrived to claim, as his slave by inheritance, a negro servant Parkyns had engaged at Adwa, and he decoyed him to his house and put him in chains. 'In truth,' Parkyns remembered, 'I think I never passed a period of my life more wretchedly than I did the few days at Howzayn.'

However, his inactivity gave him the opportunity to see what an Abyssinian army's camp was like, for it was an important institution in the life of the country.

A year later he was to become much more familiar with a camp of this kind and its occupants. At Howzayn his observation was mainly visual and he thought it 'singular, but by no means unpleasing'. He saw it with a draughtsman's eye.

The diversity of tents – some bell-shaped, some square, like an English marquee; some white, and others of the black woollen stuff; huts of all sizes and colours, and their inmates

[57]

scattered about in groups, with their horses, mules, etc., form altogether a picturesque and very lively scene.

The organization interested him too.

> In the centre is the dwelling of the Prince, which consists of three or four large thatched wigwams and a tent, enclosed by a double fence of thorns, at the entrances through which guards are stationed, the space between them being divided into courts, in which the soldiers or other persons craving an audience await his pleasure.

Around this nucleus the various functionaries and formations had their traditional places. Close to the Prince's tent were the quarters of his 'steward' with his numerous followers, used also as porters when the Prince was on the move, as collectors of forage and wood, and as soldiers when required. In camp they had various and complex duties in the service of food and drink. Nearby were the 'guards', the 'muskateers', and the 'drummers', an important group, for drums were visual and aural evidence of the Prince's status. The 'guards' were also responsible for carrying out the ghastly judicial punishments inflicted by the Prince in accordance with established practice; punishments that rivalled in severity, if not in ingenuity, anything devised by unreformed European justice.

Behind the Prince's quarters were those of the 'swordbearers'. Further behind camped the rearguards. The layout, the sedentary version of the army on the march, was by no means precise as an abbreviated description of this kind might suggest, but even on the march, the confusion was less than a European might suppose, for every soldier, through long experience, knew where his place was and what was expected of him in battle. Basically, each company of about fifty men had a leader recognizable by his hut in camp being rather larger than those of his followers who camped in a circle around it. He had usually been a favourite servant before receiving this promotion. He was expected to provide a minimum ration of food for his men, and he was entitled to maintain discipline by depriving his followers of their allowances. In brief, the system was similar to one employed by the Ottoman Turks and had the merit of simplicity. There was no time wasted on pay-sheets and paymasters, quartermasters, indents and the like. On the other hand, the army was permanently short of almost every-thing it needed, except undernourished soldiers.

Eventually the Englishmen were summoned to the presence, after waiting for a considerable time under a burning sun in the outer compound and at the door. The correct procedure for an Abyssinian on entering was to prostrate himself with his head to the ground, but a low bow sufficed for a foreigner.

> Our bow was vaguely directed, because in passing from the glare of a tropical sun at noon into an apartment lighted only by a small door, over which was suspended a curtain, and which communicated with a tent outside, it may be imagined that we could not distinguish a single object within.

To the absence of daylight was added the smoke of a wood fire.

The ceremonial was simple. Ras Oubie was in the posture appropriate to his rank, reclining on the simplest of wooden bedsteads, 'covered with a common Smyrna rug, and furnished with a couple of chintz cushions'. Parkyns thought him: 'rather a good-looking slight-made man of about forty-five years, with bushy hair which was fast turning grey'. The impression he gave was: 'more of the fox than the lion'. To Plowden's eye, the Prince was

> grave in manner, and of a piercing eye, silent and reserved, and much feared by all who approach him. He has no liveliness in his conversation and is cold to strangers, but in business quick, decided, and precise . . . He has ambition and pride in a large share . . . governs with a firm hand, and his country is wonderfully quiet.

Plowden was not far wrong. Ras Oubie was hated by most of the Tigreans he ruled, partly because he was from the province of Semien, west of the Takazze river, and did not speak the Tigrinya dialect, and partly because his rule was heavy-handed and enforced by his Amhara retainers. Even today the people of Tigré recall pejorative jingles composed around his name that have been transmitted through the generations.

What the Ras thought of his bedraggled visitors is a matter for conjecture. They bowed as they entered, and bowed again after he had made formal inquiries about their health. Then they were beckoned to be seated – on the ground, of course. Before Parkyns could see through the darkness and smoke, he found himself squatting within a yard of the fire with his eyes streaming.

I bore it with the utmost fortitude till I could endure it no longer, and then started up with an exclamation like 'Oof!' at which Oubi laughed amazingly. Great men, I suppose, require more heat than others in these countries, as I cannot otherwise account for Oubi's taste in having a large fire in the middle of August, especially in a tropical climate.

The proceedings were brief.

Our presents were brought in covered with cloths, and carried by our servants. They consisted of a Turkey rug, two European light cavalry swords, four pieces of muslin for turbans, and two or three yards of red cloth for a cloak.

They were certainly modest compared with those the Ras was used to receiving from official parties, particularly from the French in recent years. The Prince examined them, passed a complimentary remark and uttered the required phrase, 'God return it to you', which was not to be taken literally. The Ras kept the presents but ordered his stewards to give his visitors a cow. 'Such a cow!' wrote Parkyns, 'as thin as a cat – an absolute bag of bones'. It remained only to have their 'introducer' confirmed; to explain that they were merely travellers; to complain about the dues demanded by the *negad ras* at Adwa; and to take their leave. All this business could be handled by the experienced John Bell, who had been present at previous receptions at the Prince's camp two years earlier. 'We bowed,' wrote Parkyns, 'and took our departure, glad enough to re-enter our huts and prepare for our return to Adowa on the morrow'. He was glad to have done with this brief glimpse of high authority. It had been very different from what James Bruce's book, *Travels*, had led him to expect. No banquets for the consumption of raw beef and mead on an heroic scale, no orgies.

Parkyns should have been more impressed with Ras Oubie than he was. Subsequently, he became interested in the history of the Ras's career and recorded it in detail from the evidence of those who had witnessed it; but for the time being he was unable to respect men in authority unless they met his ingenuous standards. Ras Oubie fell short of them. Nevertheless, the Ras gave the Englishmen an escort for their return journey to Adwa, with instructions for the *negad ras* not to charge customs dues on Parkyns' possessions.

Their return journey went quickly and Parkyns outstripped the others. He was now aware of the advantages of travelling alone with few retainers and little baggage compared with the limitations of travelling in company with other Europeans, particularly those with commercial commitments. Equally, he was aware that he could not satisfy his interest in the people of the country, as well as its wildlife, unless he could do it in his own way, in his own time. August was passing and he must decide what use he should make of the forthcoming months of dry weather. Should he persist with his original plan for accompanying John Bell and Walter Plowden on their expedition to the Galla sources of the White Nile? As a first step towards the crossing of Africa, it was a roundabout and uncertain route to follow.

However, he did not change his mind about wanting to cross Africa, but he began to think that a shorter route to the Nile and places beyond it, with himself in charge of his fate, would be a preferable alternative to travelling with Bell and Plowden. He calculated that it might take at least two years for him to reach the Nile at Khartoum by their route. A more direct course to the west would leave him with time in hand. Moreover, he did not feel that he could leave Tigré until the letters he was expecting from England had reached him; especially until he had received more money for his immediate requirements, as well as proof that his debt to Mr Ogilvy at Jedda had been settled. In fact, it is evident that Parkyns was beginning to feel the consequences of the casual and inadequate arrangements he had made before leaving Cairo.

After the three men had reached their Adwa house once more, Plowden suffered a further attack of malaria and, when he had recovered, he went to Aksum for a change of air. This was the capital of the ancient kingdom of Abyssinia, twenty miles west of Adwa on the road to Gondar. Parkyns remained with John Bell, and from him he learned that the best place for birds and game within reasonable distance of Adwa was in the valley of the River Mareb in the district of Addi Abbo, at places about forty miles downstream from the point at which he had crossed the river on his way up from the coast. Bell had been there himself two years earlier when he volunteered to go to the rescue of two French naturalists of the Lefebvre expedition who had unwisely entered the valley too soon after the rains. He went in vain, for both Frenchmen and several of their retainers died of fever. On Bell's recommendation, Parkyns decided to set out for the Mareb Valley.

His destination was the rough country north-west of Adwa; part of Tigré but off the beaten track from Adwa to Gondar. He wrote:

> My principal object in going there was the chase, and if possible to learn something of the neighbouring Barea or Shangalla, – a race totally unknown except by the reputation they have gained in many throat-cutting visits paid to the Abyssinians . . . I was told much of the dangers I was to meet with from the climate and the people . . . My curiosity, however, was raised, and I felt that I could trust to my own prudence not to expose myself to any unnecessary danger. I have, moreover, always found that, of the perils described to a traveller before he undertakes a journey, not more than half need be believed.

He set out, 'with a few native servants', towards the end of September 1843 when rainstorms were becoming less frequent. At once his spirits rose. What could be better than to ride one's mule in the sun along tracks where everyone he met responded politely to his greetings and cast respectful glances on the firearms he and his retinue carried? By now he knew enough of the Tigrinya language to ask simple questions and to understand some of the answers: What is the name of the tiny church, 'a mere hut, perched on a small pyramidical hill', with the candelabra euphorbias growing all over it? That is St John. And the other one further on? That is the Church of the Saviour which is exactly half-way between Adwa and Aksum. And the larger one in the distance? That is St Pantaloon near Aksum; 'the church of a saint', Parkyns explains, 'formerly held in great esteem by the people; but of late years – as apparently there is a fashion in these as in all other matters – he had been much neglected'.

This is not to say that Parkyns had a full knowledge of the language, but it takes no one long to discover that peasants and herdsmen use limited vocabularies for a limited range of subjects. It is a different matter when literate people discuss matters of religion, law, politics or abstract conceptions. Being alone and accustomed to speaking foreign languages, Parkyns probably made good progress in learning Tigrinya, as he did Arabic, without approaching standards that would satisfy academic examiners. His command of Tigrinya was sufficient for his day-to-day needs in the remote villages of the Addi Abbo districts and he was probably correct in claiming that he spoke the language more fluently than other Europeans. He was not given either to boasting or exaggeration.

There is never a lack of topics for conversation among fellow-travellers by animal transport. There is plenty of time for comment and reminiscence on what they see by the way; on the condition, qualities and needs of their animals; time for exchanging greetings, news and badinage with passers-by. Having no artificial light, no tent or camp-bed, Parkyns shared the life of the local people. Soon after it was dark, he would lie down with the rest. He wore tight-fitting homespun cotton breeches, a long cloth a yard wide wound round his middle as a belt – his own was thirty-five yards long – and a sort of toga, called a *quarry*, nine feet wide by fifteen feet long, over his torso. Parkyns usually called it his 'cloth'. He explained:

> Before sleeping the men take off their belts and trousers without disarranging their cloth, which is of itself sufficient to keep them perfectly covered: and the women likewise divest themselves of their skirts. A bachelor rolls himself up in his cloth – head, feet, face, and all completely covered up. This I found at first a rather disagreeable mode of sleeping, but soon got accustomed to it. Married couples sleep in the same manner: that is, quite naked, but rolled up close together in a sort of hydropathic dry pack, or double mummy fashion. They manage this, however, very cleverly; and I have often, when sleeping in a room with two or three married couples, been astonished at the graceful manner in which they prepare their bed without in the least degree exposing their bodies.

It is easy to see that bedroom intimacy of this kind was a better place for learning a language than a schoolroom.

The road to Addi Abbo follows the watershed dividing the

[63]

catchment areas of the River Mareb, to the north, and the much larger Takazze river to the south, beyond which lies the great Semien Massif. Aksum was the first place of importance and there Parkyns experienced none of the usual problems about accommodation. The village is on the site of the ancient capital of the Aksumite kingdom and has an important Christian church. Fortunately for Parkyns, the wife of the senior civil and religious governor, or *nebrid* of Aksum, was 'a merry, good-natured old lady of fifty, who claimed a sort of relationship with me, on account of her great-grandfather having been a Greek'. She was generous with her food and had the distinction of being one of the few vintners in the country, but he found the wine, 'of a very inferior quality that leaves a dark stain on anything it may be spilt upon'.

Naturally, the antiquarian remains attracted him at Aksum and he was soon busy, in the absence of a camera, on pictures of the 'tolerably well-built square church, probably of Portuguese construction, which forms altogether a rather agreeable *coup d'oeil*, prettily situated among large trees'. This was no exaggeration, although future generations may find it difficult to believe it after Aksum has been made a fitting place for modern international tourists. Abyssinians of Parkyns' day had less regard for the antiquity of the church than for the sanctuary it gave to fugitives, a most important facility during those troubled times.

Parkyns also did a water-colour of Aksum's two most celebrated features which he described as:

> the beautiful obelisk and splendid sycamore-tree . . . both of great height, but the latter is remarkable for the extraordinary circumference of its trunk and the great spread of its branches, which cast their dark shade over such a space of ground as would be sufficient for the camp of the largest caravan. The principal obelisk is carved on the south side, as if to represent a door, windows, cornices, etc; while under the protecting arm of the venerable tree stand five or six smaller ones, without ornaments, most of which have considerably deviated from the perpendicular. Altogether they form an interesting family party.

The tree, which was for generations regarded as remarkable as the pre-Christian monolith, has now disappeared. In its day, it provided a test for spear-throwers. Only the most famous of warriors were credited with having thrown their spears over it.

On reaching the fertile plain of Selaclaca, he turned from the Gondar road to the north into a country of rocky hills and fairly well-wooded valleys. The road he followed made him appreciate the difference in interpretation that must be given in Africa to European words and terms:

> This appellation – road – may give an idea of macadamizing, with footpaths alongside, mile-stones, fences, etc.; but here the high road is only a track worn by use, and a little larger than the sheep-paths. The utmost labour bestowed on any road in this country is when some traveller, vexed with a thorn that may happen to scratch his face, draws his sword and cuts off the spray. Even this is rarely done; and I have been astonished at seeing many highways, and even some of those most used, rendered almost impassable by the number of thorns which are allowed to remain spread across them. An Abyssinian's maxim is, 'I may not pass by this way for a year again; why should I give myself trouble for other people's convenience?

To his delight, Parkyns came across several Abyssinian hornbills:

> A quaint looking bird, nearly the size of a turkey . . . The bird's throat is furnished with red and blue wattles, and the sides of the beak with a pair of black moustachios that would do credit to a hussar.

He added one to his collection.

Being his own master, he evolved his own code of behaviour as a guest in the villages through which he passed:

> Many travellers adopt the practise of taking a soldier from the chief or King of the country in which they may be travelling, to ensure them a hospitable reception in the villages where they may be obliged to lodge . . . What right has Oubi to make his peasantry feed me or anyone else? They pay their taxes, whether or no.

He was strongly opposed to the traditional soldier escort:

> In the first place, it often leads to a quarrel, which is a

disagreeable introduction into a village . . . Secondly, to have an Amhara soldier with you is no recommendation to the confidence of Tigreans . . . Thirdly, 'Every man's house is his castle'.

His own recipe was simple:

There's nothing like a civil tongue and quiet unpretending manner to get one on in these countries, as I suppose in all others. On my arrival at a village I have always found it a better plan to wait under a tree till some one asks me in. This is generally soon done, though a little patience is sometimes needed.

On this friendly basis, and with an increasing familiarity with the language, Parkyns enjoyed himself hugely.

How little are the gifts of Nature appreciated by those who, living in the midst of luxury, are accustomed only to wish for a thing in order to obtain it! Ye who have already satiated yourselves with the bounties of Providence, take my advice – leave for a time your lives of luxury, shoulder your rifle, and take a few months' experience of hardship in a hot climate. You will suffer much at first, but in the end you will learn what real enjoyment is. You will sleep soundly when you throw yourselves down on the bare ground . . . You will find more real pleasure in a draught of water, even if it be a little dirty, than you ever did in the choicest wine to be got in England. You will devour a half-burned piece of gazelle, and find it more palatable than the cuisine of the greatest gourmand in Paris . . . Shade, a bit of green grass, a rippling stream, a cloud – all these are treasures in Africa, though not cared for or heeded in a land where you have trees in every hedge-row, a velvet turf in every garden and in many fields, a river almost every three or four miles, and, as for clouds, perhaps rather too many of them.

There were no maps for him to follow, but he benefited much from the fact that very few Europeans had visited this part of the country, for he was a figure of curiosity. Moreover, with his smattering of Tigrinya, his Abyssinian dress and plaited hair, he was clearly accepted as a person of goodwill. 'I seldom rode, preferring always to walk, except after meals, or when the country was dull and uninteresting, and then I generally managed to doze on my saddle.'

Parkyns and his party arrived one evening at a village near a small waterfall.

Seeing no one about, I sat down under a tree, but had scarcely done so when the chief of the village came out, with his cloth lowered so as to leave his shoulders bare – a sign of the greatest respect and humility – and with more than European politeness upbraided me for not having entered his house at once. He conducted me to his best hut, whence he had ejected his wife and family, and, after seeing me comfortably settled, brought me a goat and some beer; and nothing that I could say would induce him to sit down, or to desist from serving me with his own hands. He had never before seen a European, nor ever heard talk of white men, excepting the Greek silversmiths at Adwa, so that it could have been from no hope of reward that he behaved thus liberally. Rain coming on towards night, I begged him to return with his family to the hut I occupied, the only waterproof one of the lot; it was with difficulty I induced him to do so, and, even when he did comply, it was with many apologies for the intrusion. Before we went to sleep he got more at ease, after having discussed the greater part of a large jar of beer, and it ended by not only himself, wife, and four children joining me in the hut, but also two donkeys, a lot of goats, and a whole tribe of fowls, a large proportion of which roosted exactly over my head.

The principal village of the Addi Abbo province is Addaro, and it was there that Parkyns met the chief of the province, Aito Merratch, who treated him kindly. In the neighbourhood he had seen a good many of Ras Oubie's soldiers, a reminder that although he was away from the main routes of the country, he was still in a place that was part of the general pattern of government, although government meant little more, as far as he could see, than the right of the strongest to impose on the rest of the population. Most of the population regarded this as normal, but Parkyns conceived a deep hatred for the 'Amhara soldiers', meaning Ras Oubie's soldiers. The soldiers sponged off the population and off him.

At Addaro, he found a decent hut to live in that was lent him by a Muslim merchant he had met on the road:

> On arriving at the town, all the inhabitants collected to have a look at me, and even after I was fairly in the house, many came peeping in at the door, though they dared not enter, from awe of the great men who were sitting with me. The children especially came running in, and, after taking one hurried but fixed stare, bolted out again, half frightened, half laughing. Many of the people had never seen a white man before.

Staying in the village for several days, he had time to observe village life more closely, and entries in his diary reflect this clearly:

> Continually bothered by visitors: really their civility waxeth disagreeable. A party of soldiers appear to relieve one another in watching over me; for as fast as one lot goes, another comes to take their place. They are always polite; but it seems to me that their politeness can scarcely be called disinterested, as it mostly ends in their insinuating that a present of some sort or another would be acceptable . . . Blessed are the swarm of bees that have lodged in the house. They have stung me several times, but I can bear that, especially as they have also stung some of my importunate visitors, who by this means are kept away. In fact, the only method I have to rid myself of my friends is to stir up the bees.

As he walked about with his inquisitive Abyssinian friends, he tried the effect of giving silly answers to silly questions.

> Is there rain in your country? I reply 'No' – Is there grass? 'No' – Is there corn? 'No' – Are there animals? 'No', then what do you eat? 'Air' – At last beginning to understand the joke, some laugh at their own folly while others go away convinced that outside Abyssinia there is nothing to eat, but that dollars are plentiful.

There was a general movement by Aito Merratch and the notables of Addaro to dissuade him from going on to the River Mareb.

He represented the dangers and difficulties I was to expect from the Barea, fevers, and even the inhabitants, whom he described as 'very good sort of people, but, like most frontier men, rather rough and lawless'. I told him that I had heard nearly a similar character of himself and his people before I left Adoua; and that, judging by the agreeable way in which I had been undeceived with regard to them and their country, I could venture to run a similar risk again.

Whereupon Parkyns' new-found friends offered:

to build me a house, and marry me to the prettiest girl in the province.

Yet, in spite of these inducements, he was determined to advance further and, early in October 1843, he set out for the district of Rohabeita, following a track that was so rough and covered with thorn bushes that even his donkeys could hardly make progress. He passed through a succession of hamlets among the rocks and hills which were to become familiar to him.

The final day's journey was short.

The road we passed over was highly picturesque, and we ended our day's work by climbing a very steep hill, the ascent to which was by means of a sort of semi-natural, semi-artificial staircase of a mile or two long. Near the top of it, however, we found a pretty little hamlet, called Addi Harisho, where we were hospitably received and comfortably lodged by the lay-dean and chief of the district, Apha-Memher Waddy-Hil.

It was in this neighbourhood that he spent the next nine months living the life of an Abyssinian frontiersman, for Rohabeita district provided exactly what he had been looking for. Even today, it is regarded as being at the back of beyond. In the past it was an area where desperate men might find hope of escape. Criminal punishments, and particularly punishments for political offences, were of a kind that made the hazards of frontier life preferable to the consequences of being caught. At the worst, a fugitive could cross the River Mareb to hide among the pagan Baria tribes who might kill him or sell him into slavery with the Egyptians in the Sudan.

[69]

Parkyns was an obvious success among these people, many of them outlaws. He was not involved in the feuds and vendettas which complicated interdistrict and interprovincial relations, large or small. In other words, his actions were not affected by family and tribal loyalties. He and his party were well armed and his men under control, in comparison with Ras Oubie's undisciplined Amharic-speaking soldiers who battened on to the villages. Also, he identified himself with the people he lived with; shared their houses, drank with them, danced with them, went on raids with them, sat as a member of their local judiciary and took the prettiest girl in the village as his wife. Moreover, he lived up to the expectation these frontiersmen had of a European; or at least the caricature of European prowess presented by those who told tales of wonder about them. He could shoot straight, ride well, bewilder with a sword, and generally display athletic prowess. James Bruce had achieved a similar reputation when he was in the country in the previous century, and his mentioning it in his book was treated by critics as an example of his petty conceit. Yet it was these qualities for which he was still remembered in the country half a century later; apart from the apocryphal story that he had found much gold and taken it away with him.

It is not to be supposed that life in the Rohabeita district was as idyllic as Parkyns' diary suggests. He wrote of it retrospectively after he left the country, and in less congenial surroundings. Nevertheless, the nine months he spent there, and the ensuing year elsewhere in Tigré, were happy ones for him, and constituted an episode in his life that he never forgot:

> Anyone who has tasted the sweets of savage life will always look back with longing to them . . . That a man brought up in the middle of civilization and refinement should presume to look back on the time he passed among savages, without society, without even a book of any sort to refresh his memory, as one of the happiest periods of his life, would to many be the equivalent to acknowledging himself possessed of a coarse and unintellectual mind.

This was indeed the judgement of many if not most of his contemporaries, but their descendants have come to feel differently.

6

The village of Addi Harisho became Parkyns' temporary home. From it, the views of the countryside were wide and splendid. He could reach an even higher point after an hour's walk, at a small thatched church named after St Theodore, which was supported by 'a few shrivelled monks'. The church was built on an isolated part of a cliff, of which two sides were precipices falling to gullies on either side; the third side, on the north, dropped sheer towards the Mareb Valley far below, with range upon range of rugged hill country beyond. The remaining side gave access to the hamlet by a gentler slope. Parkyns wrote:

> Nothing can exceed the magnificence of the view which this position commands glancing over the dark green of the uncultivated but fertile valley, through the middle of which the river, as seen from that distance, appears like a winding silver thread . . . In the extreme distance may be seen the mountains beyond Adowa, which in colour appear like faint blue clouds on the horizon, though, from the clearness of the atmosphere, their outline loses none of its distinctness even at so great a distance.

Here Parkyns could sit in the sun eyeing the prospect before him, idly talking to the monks and his companions. Their voices, hollow in the surrounding void, were the only sounds other than the remote call of a shepherd, the bleat of a goat or the screech of an eagle.

On the face of the high rock there was a cave in which the church's patron saint was said to have lived, although it was hardly big enough for a person to squat in. The monks showed him the marks worn in the rock by the crown of St Theodore's head, and soles of his feet and his elbows. They had many stories about the saint's miracles. After a leopard had eaten one of his young relations, Saint Theodore set out to rescue him. He shouted in the forest so commandingly that the leopard appeared with the young relation half-digested inside him. 'Nevertheless, so great was the Saint's power,' Parkyns was assured, 'that the boy left the leopard's maw none the worse for having been dismembered and reconstructed.' Perhaps rather the better, Parkyns added.

However, reveries of this kind, and gossiping with his Abyssinian companions, were only incidental to his collecting bird specimens and other objects of natural history in the Mareb Valley. He could reach it from the village down a steep track over the hot boulders that, when the sun was at its zenith, looked from a distance as if they had a coating of oil. One of the best places for birds was an intermediate piece of flat ground on the floor of the valley but above the bed of the river. The rocky hills rose steeply from it on both sides, and it was hot and silent. He spent much of his time there; among the tall grass, thin bush and the mimosa trees. Apart from the birds, it was visited

by buffaloes and elephant and several kinds of antelope. The beautiful sunbirds and others flit about the sweet-scented blossoms of the mimosa; while parrots and the long-tailed parroquets, whistling, pass in flights from one large tree to another. Eagles and hawks of many species come down from the hills in quest of prey, and nearly all the varieties belonging to the low, hot climates of Abyssinia are to be met with.'

By the river, no more than a series of stagnant pools in the dry season, he was able to tickle fish among the rocks. The local people poisoned, or rather stupified them with the milky excretion from the giant euphorbias. There were tracks of wild animals and birds of all kinds for him to identify. As he put it:

from the fine sand by the water's edge may be studied the different forms of feet of the reptorial, natatorial, grallatorial, or insessional orders, better than in any book of ornithology.

It was a splendid field for a naturalist and clearly he worked diligently. The stories he heard from his Abyssinian companions threw light on their relations with the animals that played such a prominent part in their lives; an attitude very different from that of his European contemporaries. He felt that he should give some explanation for not having shot more game; particularly lions. A dead lion was the badge of the Victorian Nimrod; yet Parkyns confessed that:

> I never killed a lion during all my stay in Africa – I perhaps should have done so, if I had known what a fuss is made about it at home; but in Abyssinia it is not an easy thing to accomplish . . . I never once heard a native hunter of these parts say that he had seen or heard of a lion's den . . . these animals lived during the day among the inaccessible rocks and jungle, but at no fixed place.

Mostly, Parkyns had glimpses of them at night, but he got tired of losing his sleep waiting up for one of them. In due course:

> you politely request him to take himself off to a certain warm place, and, returning your rifle between your legs, roll over and go to sleep. . . . Some people may think that this is a queer place for a rifle; but, on the contrary, it is the position of all others wherein utility and comfort are most combined. The butt rests on the arm, and serves as a pillow for the head; the muzzle points between the knees, and the arms encircle the lock and breech; so that, besides having a smooth pillow, the butter from your hair is beneficially employed in toughening the wood, instead of being lost on a stone, while you are always prepared to start up armed at a moment's notice.

We must take his word for it. Francis Galton recommended the position in his book *The Art of Travel* and doubtless many imaginative young Victorians wrestled with their firearms as a result.

However, there were plenty of lions in the valleys of the major rivers of Abyssinia and in the remoter frontier hills, even if Parkyns did not get a shot at them. He found that:

> The natives of these parts do not hold the lion in such dread as one would be led to believe by the accounts of some travellers . . . They have an idea here that, if attacked with metal weapons, such as spears, swords, or guns, the lion will turn on his assailants: but that he will invariably take himself off if sticks and stones only be employed against him.

Similarly, they thought that a lion took three leaps before seizing its victim and that if the lion's third leap could be avoided he would not attempt a second attack: 'this theory is very little to be relied on,' Parkyns observed. In the Galla country, his companions told him, there was a tribe in which the boys killed lions single-handed. Their method was that

> the boy provokes the kingly animal by insulting epithets, till he springs open mouthed at him, when, with great dexterity, the youthful hunter thrusts his pointed stick between the lion's jaws which is thereby rendered innocuous, after which the boy proceeds deliberately to cut the lion's throat with his knife.

No one seemed to disbelieve the story, and Parkyns soon found that fanciful legends of this kind – tribesmen with tails, crocodiles that wept, men who turned into hyenas, and so on – were a way in which these illiterate people exercised their imaginations and amused themselves in conversation. The imagination and the tongue are the most portable instruments of artistic expression and are always available to people who have no mechanical devices. Parkyns also learned to discount even the more credible stories if they were related to anything or anyone so far distant that direct inquiries about them could not be made. It was the remoteness of Europe that gave trans-Saharan Africans a belief in European magical powers. One man – an itinerant Sudanese scribe – told Parkyns that he knew very well how strangers were treated in Europe. 'I asked him "How?" "Why," said he, "they hang them up by the legs, and then flog them with whips, and the sweat which falls from them under this treatment, being collected and cooled, becomes corrosive sublimate!" '

In spite of his armament and his proficiency as a shot,

Parkyns was mainly interested in the pacific study of wildlife:

The ravine down which the brook fell was well wooded, and the trees were filled with . . . a beautiful species of little greenish-grey monkey, with black face and white whiskers. I followed a troop of these for a long time . . . not at all with the intention of hurting them, but merely for the pleasure of watching their movements. If you go tolerably carefully towards them they will allow you to approach very near . . . You may see them quarrelling, making love, mothers taking care of their children, combing their hair, nursing and suckling them; and the passions – jealousy, anger, love – as fully and distinctly marked as in men. They have a language as distinct to them as ours is; and their *women* are as noisy and fond of disputation as any fish-fag in Billingsgate.

Similarly he observed, with acuteness and originality, the habits of baboons, leopards, crocodiles, hippos, buffaloes, hyenas, jackals, wild dogs, various gazelles and antelopes, hares, conies, and

an animal called 'saheyra' which I could not obtain, of which the Abyssinians have some curious ideas; it lives in holes in the ground, and is said to feed on dead bodies, etc., coming out only at night.

As for birds, he collected some three hundred varieties, including a vulture with an eleven-foot wing-span:

ten or twelve sorts of eagles . . . twenty-four sorts of hawks and falcons, many of them very interesting . . . several kinds of plovers, six of grouse and partridge; two very handsome geese, and five sorts of ducks.

The list was longer still, and his collection rewarding, for the Mareb Valley had a great variety of very beautiful birds. 'There are ten or eleven sorts of cuckoo, one of which, the emerald cuckoo' – presumably he referred to *Coccopygia melanotis*, or Yellow-bellied Waxbill – 'though nearly the smallest, may be reckoned the most beautiful bird in this part of Africa, from the brilliant green of its back, contrasted with the bright yellow of its breast.' One can understand how his retainers were kept busy preparing and preserving bird-skins; about twelve hundred, Parkyns thought.

His dress while he was at work in the Mareb Valley was simple and practical:

> My dress on these occasions consisted of a short kilt of nicely tanned antelope hide, a piece of coarse cotton cloth wrapped round my waist by day as a belt and used as a covering at night, and a small wild cat's or jackal's skin thrown over the left shoulder. Add to these a kid-skin filled with flour, a little horn of cayenne pepper and salt mixed, and a small piece of thin leather for a bed, and you have all the wardrobe, kitchen, and furniture which an Abyssinian frontier-man thinks necessary for a fortnight's outlying . . . St. John the Baptist's living on locusts and wild honey is easily understood by anyone who has been in these countries.

Fortunately his health remained good, although some of his ideas were unconventional; he never wore a hat and he ate anything available: 'every living thing that walketh, flieth, or creepeth . . . Still I cannot manage the game, "Just properly kept", so much esteemed by epicures in England'.

On medical treatment his ideas were Spartan. He was averse to general bleedings, but:

> Local bleedings, such as the natives practice, are most highly advantageous; and firing with a red hot iron at their recommendation may also be adopted. For severe inflammation of the bowels, when you cannot bear to be touched on the part, some boiling water poured on it will be a ready and effective blister.

It is hardly surprising that he should add: 'With all these modes of treatment, if you have the means, take internally twenty-five to thirty drops of laudanum, and a similar quantity of the liquid ammonia'.

Wounds healed rapidly, and this Parkyns also attributed to an abstemious diet. Mostly he went barefoot, on an excruciatingly hostile surface of hot rock, gravel and coarse sand. He recalled:

> On one or two occasions I remember being astonished at the little I suffered from otherwise ugly wounds about the feet. Once I struck my foot against an edge of rock which was as sharp as a razor, and a bit of flesh, with the whole of the nail

of my left foot little toe was cut off . . . I could not stop longer than to polish off the bit which was hanging by a skin, for we were in chase of a party of Barea, who had cut the throats of three of Wady Hil's nephews the night before, and I was obliged to go on running for about twenty miles that afternoon, the greater part of the way in burning sand. Whether this cured it I know not, but I scarcely suffered at all from it next day, and forgot it the day after.

On another occasion his foot was pierced by a wooden splinter the size of a ten inch nail. He walked two miles and extracted it with a nail-wrench, explaining:

with the exception of a little stiffness for a day or two, which nowise prevented my walking, I suffered no pain at all. Now had this occurred to me in Europe, and under a good European diet, I should have been at least a fortnight laid up with a bad foot.

As for thorns:

I thought no more of picking half a dozen out of my feet than an English sportsman would of kicking away the clod of clay he may have accumulated on his shooting-boots in crossing a soft ploughed field.

To the simple people of Rohabeita district he must have seemed excessively interested in birds and animals which were ordinary to them. What made Parkyns acceptable was his readiness to share their lives; sometimes to excess. Before he left the district, he joined with such zeal in putting out a fire roaring among the tinder-dry grass huts that the side of his face was severely burnt and the sight of his right eye permanently impaired. He gained also a considerable reputation for bravery.

In spite of the time he gave to his work as an amateur naturalist, Parkyns also took care to inquire into, and record, all he observed about the manners and customs of the people. Anthropology was still in its infancy in Europe and Parkyns had received no instruction in the subject. Yet his observations were both penetrating and well recorded, and they were worthy of more attention than they received. European travellers in

Africa in the nineteenth century were, generally speaking, more interested in geography, economic prospects and themselves, than in Africans as 'the sons of Adam'. Many of those at home who read his account of his anthropological observations thought them, as Dr Charles Beke put it, to be 'full of obscenities, and clothed in barely decent language'. Richard Burton had not yet put pen to paper in this field.

To the chapter in his book that contains his account of his direct observations of the conduct of the Abyssinians he lived with, Parkyns originally intended to give the heading of 'Morals, Character, etc.'. He wrote:

> 'I thought necessary to preface it in this way, in order to point out that the opinion one may form of a people from a few glaring instances of crime, or even of valour or benevolence, ought not to be criterions for the entire nation.'

He did not exempt himself from lapses of this kind but he added, with justification, that the more a person assimilates himself to the people of the country, 'the less likely he is to form a false opinion of their dispositions'.

He himself carried assimilation to the point of taking a temporary wife and establishing his own home, a procedure common in Abyssinia where the solemnizing of marriage in a church was readily circumvented. For obvious reasons, he made no mention of this in his book, but in his diary, written for his family in England, he hinted at it in a romantic passage written after he had left the country. For some time he had been offered wives, mainly because his Abyssinian hosts were uncertain about the wisdom of having a bachelor in their houses. Among them was his tipsy host at Rohabeita, the fugitive chieftain Waddy Hil whose custom it was to entertain in honour of St Michael on his feast-day. This involved the building of a rectangular hut out of straw and green boughs of trees, to act as a dining hall. In preparation, everyone was busy for a few days before the festival in brewing the local beer, making mead from the plentiful honey, baking unleavened bread, bringing in animals for slaughter, and so on. Expectations were aroused in the small community which, when it assembled for its carouse, included priests and scribes, some soldiers and the women, and visitors from neighbouring villages. Many of them had spent the previous evening and night praying, dancing and drinking in the little church of St Theodore on the precipice. Few were sober when they arrived at the party in the village.

Parkyns himself had been down in the Mareb Valley and did not arrive until late in the afternoon. He recalled:

> On entering, the spoony-sentimental way in which I was welcomed by all the party – men and women coming forward by dozens to embrace me – was at once a proof that they were all very drunk. I went and sat down by Waddy Hil. He said little, but from the peculiarly facetious smile which accompanied whatever he did say, even when discussing the most serious subjects, I soon saw that he was but little better than his neighbours.

Before the evening was out, the guests had come to blows: 'a most undignified pugilistic encounter between a very short and thick scribe and a long elephant-hunter, a most singular pair for a duel'.

Parkyns was otherwise engaged, for it was on this occasion that he met his temporary wife, Tures.

> Still I remember that eve and many a year must pass before I can cease to remember the cause which has fixed so firmly the feast of St. Michael on my memory. It was then that I first met a friend whom I have had reason to forget, not a friend of a day but one whose attachment was tried through all my stay in Abyssinia, nearly two years, as a friend whose sincerity and attachment and as a servant whose devotion and fidelity might well set aside the prejudices which vain Europeans have against a skin a little darker than our own, and proved that the colour of the heart very often depends nothing on that of the skin. Such are the great difficulties which wanderers like I have to encounter: Leave to those who boast of the personal dangers and sufferings they have had to encounter, the glory of having overcome them, give to me only the credit of the courage and prudence necessary to separate myself from scenes and persons rendered dear to me by long attachment and that affection for my home and family which alone can suffice to console me on such a separation.

Leaving aside the sentimental memories of a lonely young

man, the importance of this liaison was that it committed Parkyns to an even closer identity with the people he was among. It was no novelty for a European to take an Abyssinian wife, and civil marriages of this kind, recognized as being essentially temporary, were not frowned on locally. Indeed, the Abyssinian women attached considerable prestige to bearing children by white Christian fathers, or so Europeans believed. Some say that it was a tradition that originated with the Portugese expeditions in the sixteenth century. Clearly it gave Parkyns a special opportunity for learning more of the Tigrinya language and it enabled him to write with greater authority on the domestic customs of the people of northern Abyssinia.

By tradition, Tures is credited with 'noble descent': certainly her father was related to Tigrean chieftains and, on the physical evidence of her descendants, she had a light complexion and good looks. Parkyns' liaison with her did not mean that he exchanged his rough life for domestic indolence. On the contrary, his inquisitiveness led him further afield to study the tribes of negro Baria beyond the Mareb; in the province now known as Eritrea.

Like any other European visitor to northern Abyssinia, Parkyns soon became aware of the word 'Baria', although there was some confusion over the exact meaning of the word. 'Baria' denoted a negroid and pagan tribe on the northern frontier of the country, that preyed on the Christian population with cunning, ruthlessness and brutality. More accurately, the word 'Baria' denotes 'slaves'.

Parkyns was also aware of the unenviable position of the primitive Barea in relation to their Christian neighbours to the north. Both Christians and Muslims were permitted to own slaves, provided the slaves were not taken from tribes that were co-religionists. So the Baria, and other pagan peoples, were an obvious source of supply. On the other hand, the Baria had no compunction about selling Christians they captured as slaves to their Muslim neighbours in the Sudan. Consequently a state of perpetual hostilities existed between the Baria and their neighbours.

When Parkyns was living in the Rohabeita district in 1843 and 1844, pressure on the Baria was beginning to take a more modern form, although their fate had been clear enough ever since the Abyssinians of Tigré province acquired firearms. The position had become worse for them since 1840, when a Turco-Egyptian expedition from Khartoum occupied the area north-west of the Baria, known as Taka. There the Egyptians established an administrative centre and garrison at Kassala. And so, the Baria was sandwiched between the Egyptians and the Abyssinians, African states that were to assume 'imperialist characteristics' in their mutual jealousies over this frontier many years before the arrival of European imperialism. The Baria suffered, first, because they were pagans – an unforgivable offence to their Muslim and Christian neighbours; secondly, because they usually wore no clothes, which was just as offensive; and, thirdly, because they committed the ultimate offence of defending themselves from being either slaughtered, enslaved or clothed.

Naturally, Parkyns' attitude to the Baria was conditioned by the Abyssinians amongst whom he was living. They were at war with the Baria, not only in the Mareb Valley but also in the Abyssinian villages in the hills above it, where the people had learnt to be on the alert against Baria attacks and ambushes. One day, Parkyns was seeing off a friend:

I accompanied him some distance on the road with a small party of our people, as he had been alarmed when coming by signs of Barea. He said that he and all with him were confident that the blacks were outlying on the road . . . Scarcely had we passed the brook at Mai-Chena when one of our men, a hunter, declared that he saw the slaves. Being at that time inexperienced in such matters, I could see nothing suspicious. He then pointed out to me a dead tree standing on an eminence at a distance of several hundred yards, and charred black by last year's fire . . . All that I saw was a charred stump of a tree, and a few blackened logs and stones lying at its feet. The hunter declared that neither the tree nor the stones were there the last time he passed, and that they were simply naked Barea, who had placed themselves in that position to observe us . . . I could scarcely believe it possible that they should remain so motionless, and I determined to explore at little . . . A shot from my rifle, at a long distance, acted on the tree and stones as powerfully as the fiddle of Orpheus, but with the contrary effect; for the tree

[81]

disappeared, and the stones and logs, instead of running after me, ran in the opposite direction. I was never more astonished in my life . . . Next day we returned to the spot and scoured the whole country, but to no purpose, although traces, not only of the enemy's footmarks, but also of their camp fires, were plainly visible.

Alarms of this kind were not infrequent, and Parkyns accompanied one or two raids that the people of Rohabeita organized against the Baria, either to find people who were missing, or for purposes of reprisal. On one occasion, Parkyns recalled, 'I was just taking a sort of stirrup-cup with old chief Waddy Hil, my mule standing saddled outside the hut, and my men waiting, when I heard a loud wail from a distance'. They all hurried off to a hamlet on a neighbouring hill. The screaming was so loud that they supposed an attack was in progress but, on arrival, they found that the place had not actually been attacked but that two men, 'highly respectable' Parkyns called them, had failed to return from a visit to their cultivations.

The pursuit lasted for two days but Parkyns did not conceive a high regard of his Abyssinian friends' skill or courage. 'The more enterprising and ambitious among them seemed to be interested mainly in obtaining some part of their enemies' anatomy, taken from the dead or living, to bring back with them as a trophy', he wrote. Formalized boasting of warlike achievements played an important part in Abyssinian morale and self-expression. Consequently, bravery was not always related to battle: much of it was displayed in pantomime at a safe distance from the enemy. While Parkyns and his friends on this occasion were engaged in their unsuccessful pursuit of the Baria marauders, he recalled that:

I never saw such valour displayed. It was really quite wonderful. One man was to take two trophies, another three; none talked of prisoners, all were so very bloodthirsty . . . I felt as brave as anyone. But, to tell the truth, we none of us thought it at all probable, or even possible, that we should come up with our chase, or really I don't know whether we should have been quite so gloriously disposed. Once or twice, when one of the party fancied he saw something ahead, we all became rather more mercifully inclined . . . I wish I had some fine story to dilate upon of a desperate fight, wherein I

Mansfield Parkyns as a child on his grandmother's lap

Mansfield Parkyns as a young man

Watercolour scenes of Abyssinia by Mansfield Parkyns
Above: Camels racing
Below: A pair of Abba Goumba birds

Watercolour scenes of Abyssinia by Mansfield Parkyns
Above: Abyssinian warriors
Below: A typical village scene

Above: View of the obelisk and church at Axum
Below: View on the banks of the Tacazze

Emma Louise, Mansfield
Parkyns' wife with one of their
daughters

John Parkyns, the Ethiopian
son of Mansfield Parkyns

Woodborough Hall and its gardens. Mansfield Parkyns (wearing the white bowler hat) with friends and family

Mansfield Parkyns in his old age

. . . had done deeds worthy of a Bayard or an Admirable Chrichton. Alas! I have none such to tell. The only rencontres which I could relate would in nowise either amuse my readers or reflect any credit on any person connected with the victors, being for the most part retaliations, wherein a few men were butchered and mutilated by often ten times their numbers . . . But as for interest, I should hope that few of my countrymen would consider the descriptions of such scenes as more agreeable than would be that of the decapitation of a criminal, or some peculiar mode of butchering animals.

For Parkyns, who was no more squeamish than any other country-bred young man of his generation in England, it was a glimpse of life in Africa that was not seen by many European visitors. Of course, the butchering of a Baria marauder in the Mareb Valley was not materially different from the victim's point of view from the bayoneting of a scarlet-coated European soldier on a European battlefield, but most Europeans of the period did not see it in this way. To them, African killings were evidence of savagery; European casualties in battle had an aura of heroism.

For Parkyns, the Baria had a number of characteristics of which he approved:

The Barea are very brave, strong, active, and hardy, and were they a little more civilised or were they to unite in any force, would prove very dangerous enemies to Tigre. Still, however, I doubt if civilization, unless carried out to its fullest extent, improves a savage race in any particular . . . In regard to any acquaintance with modern improvements in the art of killing their fellow men they are remarkably wanting. For instance, they fear horsemen very much less than foot soldiers, imagining that the former must be old or infirm men who, not being able to keep up with their comrades on foot, require to be carried by horses; while in reality, an Abyssinian who owns a horse must be either a rich man, or a distinguished warrior, whom his chief has rewarded with the gift of one.

They were unaccustomed to firearms, and when hit by a bullet they did not connect the explosion at a distance with the wound inflicted. Parkyns saw them pushing fingers into their wounds to find out what had caused them.

The cool winter weather was over. The 'little rains' early in 1844 had fallen. Parkyns had been so fully occupied that he had not attached much significance to the absence of any communication with the outside world. Instead, he began to contemplate remaining in the Rohabeita district 'until at least I had done some little good to my poor people, and arranged matters with them, so as to leave them in comparative security'. He had asked his family to send him £300 and his plan was to lend this at the rate of £2 each to the men of the village to buy ploughs, oxen, and seeds. The improved yields of future harvests would enable them to reimburse this and to repay any grain he might have supplied to them during the first year. 'Thus, at the expiration of two years, up to which time I should have required no taxes, they would have been in comfortable circumstances, and able to look forward to a chance of ameliorating their condition.'

He anticipated that the good reputation of his administration would attract young men from elsewhere who wanted to make their fortune. These he would train as soldiers and he would also require resident house-holders to send a quota of young men to join him in lieu of paying taxes. The resulting corps would then be used to resist the attacks of the Baria and

> make forays into their country, and bring home as much profit as they could in ivory and buffalo-hides. The spoils thus procured would, according to the custom of the country, have been divided between the hunter and myself, as the owner of the guns, ammunition, etc., and my share would have been amply sufficient to make up for the loss of tax, which the family of the hunter would have failed to pay me that year, besides that he would also have been in the way of enriching himself.

He was not unaware of the hazards of trusting the men he had to deal with as partners in a business of this kind, but he proposed to have 'direction and surveillance of some experienced and trustworthy officer, who would have a certain interest in my gains'. All innocent, boyish ideas, but the expression of someone with a warm heart and good intentions who had, if the truth be told, not the least illusions that his plans would fructify.

So he passed his time in exploring the district in detail, planning sites for new villages, schemes for their defence, and a suitable place for his own house. For the rest of his life he remembered Rohabeita 'as a sort of' "Happy Valley", with all the necessary enjoyments and none of the drawbacks of the one described by Samuel Johnson'. Was this genuine, or was he finding an excuse for his conduct? He was too honest to deceive.

The climate was wretchedly bad at certain seasons of the year, the accommodation rather inferior to that possessed by our gipsies, and for whole months I have tasted nothing beyond the produce of the chase (i.e. game and honey) and a little of the coarse dagousha bread and capsicums. I can remember running in the heat of the day near two miles up a hill feasting my imagination on raw onions which my servant procured from a neighbouring village, with the greedy haste of a schoolboy who hears of a box of good things from his mama. Even milk was very scarce, only one milch cow being found in the neighbourhood, and she left us.

If Rohabeita was inferior in these respects to the Happy Valley, it was commendable 'in the innocent, peaceful life which the inhabitants led towards one another'. Parkyns himself enjoyed 'the esteem and affection in which I am sure I was held by my neighbours, and which I most sincerely reciprocated to them'. Summing up his feelings about his stay in the Rohabeita district, he wrote in his journal a year later:

Perhaps it was rather an animal than an intellectual life which I led, but after all, it was a life of peace and innocence and a life which suits so unambitious a person as myself. I have often thought how happy I could be, could I make up my mind to return and live in these primitive countries, as a sort of petty chief with my fife and drums and all the little appurtenances of their childish show, but loved and respected by all my neighbours and friends and perhaps of some little use to them. Many a time have I picked out the spot where to build a hut and planned the repair of the little church on the rocks, and add to greatness by endowing it with a bell. I heard that one of the best in the country cost the enormous sum of £2–14ˢ, and thought that very dear, considering how many cows it was equivalent to, and then, awakening from my reverie, I remembered that I was an Englishman and laughed at myself.

Many an isolated young European since Parkyns' day has indulged himself with similar fantasies when representing one side of the meeting of Europe and Africa. Few have confessed it, and fewer still have failed to acknowledge the practicalities of a problem that can only be solved in terms of generations and not without damage. Parkyns woke up to an increasing anxiety to hear news from home and, in June 1844, he set out on the return journey to Adwa to obtain it.

7

The small procession that Mansfield Parkyns led into Adwa in
June 1844 resembled that of any Abyssinian squire on the
move, except for the efficiency of its armament. Its leader was
well turned-out, for Parkyns was always fastidious in his dress,
whether English or African, and his hair was now long enough
to have it plaited and lubricated with sheep's fat. Men on foot
carried his firearms before him. Behind, were others carrying
his round shield, and their swords and spears. Presumably, his
wife Tures was on a mule at a suitable distance. He hired a
house in the Salaamji quarter from *blatta* Sahli; *blatta* being an
honorific title equivalent to 'page', given to minor court functionaries.

In describing the house, he commented once more on his
dislike for urban life compared with 'the more genial solitude of
the backwoods'. One can well understand why he thought so,
although his house was one of the better residences in Adwa.
Within a compound entered through a rough gate with a
porter's lodge next to it were a few grass huts, and a single room
of stone in which he slept, ate, and received guests. The stable
for his mules opened into it. 'The mules', he explained, 'stand
with their heads towards me, and when I am eating make eyes
at me'. Off the room was the *medeb*;

a sort of couch, made of stones and plastered over with mud. This is separated from my apartment by a partition wall, in which is an opening . . . The 'medeb' is used by the ladies as a withdrawing room; and from behind the curtain they peep at all that is going on in the reception hall upon festive occasions.

However, the architectural terminology may be deceptive, and it is better to judge the house from the drawing he made of it.

What troubled him most was the absence of news from England and the failure to reach him of the money and supplies he had ordered. Writing to Richard Milnes in August, he complained:

This is the 4th letter I have written to you without any answer . . . Thanks to the different consuls on the Red Sea I have now lived on charity for 5 months (i.e. on loans) and that's a pretty tale for a Parkyns to tell . . . Pray trouble yourself to write 3 words to my brother; to say that I am in Purgatory, and only want a little of my own money to get me out . . . I wish I could for only once transport myself and dine with you in London.

He was more homesick than depressed and he suffered, as so many have done in similar circumstances, from the expectations and disappointments of waiting for news. Any party of traders from Massawa, commissioned by Angelo Bracha, might have the letters he wanted, and one can well imagine that he inquired anxiously from each as it arrived. His facetiousness was not completely repressed. He enquired of Milnes:

Are you not yet Prime Minister or Secretary of State . . . What will you make of me if I do something rather 'distingué? . . . If thou be'est indeed my friend send me thy works if published with thy portrait, or cut out of the Times some of those thy speeches which have raised British oratory to a Ciceronian pitch and I will send thee in turn whatever thou willest of the wealth of Ethiopia, (which is d—d poverty).

At the same time, he wanted to assure Milnes that he was still determined to carry out his plan for crossing Africa. 'I shall in four or five months', he told him, 'start for Sennar (on the Nile) and thence, Inshallah, pass over to the Guinea coast'.

[88]

In these straitened circumstances, by his standards, Parkyns settled down to enjoy life in Tigré, as best he could.

> I was leading the life of an Abyssinian gentleman 'about town', my hair well tressed; in dull weather setting fashions, disputing and deciding on the merits and demerits of shields and spears; in fine weather swelling about the town with a quarter of a pound of butter melting on my head, face, neck and clothes, and with a tail of half-a-dozen well got-up and equally greasy soldiers at my heels; doing the great man, with my garment well over my nose at every festival and funeral worth attending; 'Hanging out' extensively when I had a few shillings to spend; sponging on my neighbours when, as was oftener the case, I had nothing: – in fact, living a most agreeable life on a very limited income.

One thing he learnt was that Abyssinian men had as strong a sense of fashion and style in their clothes and equipment as the men of other countries. Clothes generally were simple enough, consisting of homespun breeches and a white cotton 'toga' about fifteen feet long and seven feet wide with coloured bands some three inches broad at both ends; but there were various qualities of material, different coloured bands and different ways of wearing the 'toga' or *quarry* as it was called in Tigré. These variations, together with ornaments and mountings for weapons, gave an opportunity, for example, for soldiers to cut more dashing figures than civilians, although it was otherwise difficult to distinguish between their appearances.

Parkyns let it be known that he was a soldier, and he made an effort to be the best dressed and the most fashionable man in the place. He was still in his twentieth year. Describing the trousers, roughly resembling Indian jodhpurs, he explained that one version – called *càlliss* – reached half-way down the calf of the leg; and another – *coumta* – ended three inches above the knee.

> Both, if the wearer be a dandy, are made skin-tight . . . One year it may be the fashion to have the seam at the side of the 'càlliss', below the knee, of about two inches long only; while another year it will be lengthened to six or eight inches. The last was the measure at which I left it. This, however, was considered so very ultra-fashionable, that, except Dejatch Shetou, myself, and one or two others, few dared to attempt

it. It was I and my friend Shehtou who first introduced the habit of allowing the sword to swing perpendicularly from the side, instead of its sticking out horizontally, like a dog's tail . . . These, with the increased length of trousers, reaching as we wore them to nearly the ankle, and so tight below that it took an hour to draw them over the heel, gave a very 'Fast' look, and were much patronised by 'Young Abyssinia', though invariably decried by respectable elderly gentlemen.

Despite his obvious enjoyment of the primitive life, Parkyns was far from being blind to its defects, nor was he unaware of the educational limitations which prevented their amelioration.

The only education available was that provided by the churches to prepare or rather to condition a large number of children for a life of subservience to a form of Christianity that was culturally petrified.

Parkyns could hardly claim to speak with authority on questions of education, and his ideas in this respect were wishful rather than practical. It was unusual for European travellers of the time, apart from missionaries, to give attention to the subject. 'Nations', wrote Parkyns, 'are usually proud in proportion to their ignorance'. Most of the literate people in Abyssinia – priests and deacons – did not, he decided, understand what they read. The few that did had to be careful to conceal any individual ideas they might form as a result.

> Even suppose one man in a thousand could be found who had not only sufficient good sense and exemption from prejudice, but also honesty enough to declare it to his own detriment, no one would dare to follow his example, for he would at once be placed in a sort of quarantine, an excommunication of the most terrible kind being declared not only on himself, but on anyone who might enter his house or hold conversation with him, or even supply him with the common necessaries of life.

He thought an important advance could be made 'by weakening, and eventually destroying, the power of the priesthood and of superstition. To do any good here, the first step must be, by means of education, to teach the people to think'.

He had no fancy ideas about how this could be done; his approach was pragmatic:

> Money might be advantageously expended in sending out Europeans to teach them trades, and in opening schools – at first entirely under the superintendence of native masters, and without introducing European notions of religion: by inducing young men of influence among them to visit foreign lands . . . In fact, any means of enlarging their minds and gaining the affections, without alarming the prejudices, or awakening the jealousies of the Church.

These were his mature reflections while he was writing *Life in Abyssinia*. At Adwa, in 1844, he was still collecting the experience on which they were founded. Nevertheless his ideas represented one of the ways in which the country might adjust itself to its inevitable contacts with Europe and the rest of the world. Some observers, but not modern Ethiopian nationalists, have judged that the country would have made the adjustment with less suffering had it experienced a period of European administration to expedite the spread of education, economic development and governmental technical services. Writing at the time of the Italian conquest of the country in 1936, Arnold Toynbee commented: 'The spectacle presented by the one African state, apart from Liberia, that retained its complete independence, was perhaps the best justification that could be found for the partitioning of Africa among the European Powers'. Unhappily, the Italian Fascists' ideas on the enlightenment of Abyssinia were far removed from Mansfield Parkyns' youthful visions.

News of the murder of some priests on the Baria frontier persuaded Ras Oubie to undertake a punitive expedition into their territory. After the rains of 1844, he moved his camp from Howzayn to a site about two miles outside Adwa, and Parkyns went there in the hope of obtaining permission to accompany the expedition across the River Mareb. Already he had made the acquaintance of Dejaj Shehtou, one of Ras Oubie's sons, and he hoped that no objections would be raised, but his official 'introducer' let him down and the expedition left without him. It had been his intention to cross into one of the Christian districts – Dembelas, for example – that were regarded as semi-independent from Ras Oubie, in so far as they did not pay taxes to him unless they were compelled to do so. From Dembelas, on the western slopes of what is now referred to as 'the Eritrean plateau', he hoped to enter the Baria territory further west in a peaceful manner. But Ras Oubie's expedition put an end to his plan.

Instead, he had to be content with interrogating a Baria prisoner; with disappointing results. In the meantime, Ras Oubie's force, in considerable strength, marched through the area in which Parkyns had spent the previous year. It crossed the River Mareb, and formed a camp to the north of it; with Dejaj Shehtou, Parkyns' friend, commanding another camp further in advance. Parties were then sent out in various directions 'to kill, take, burn, destroy, etc., wherever, and whatever of the enemy might fall in their way'. Parkyns heard many anecdotes of their experiences and atrocities, presumably from Dejaj Shehtou. Parkyns wrote:

> In all, Dejaj Wubie stayed nearly two months in the 'slave country', which he completely traversed – so completely, I believe, as to have committed, either intentionally or by mistake, some depredations in the border villages of the more northern tribes, which are claimed as tributaries of the Egyptian Government.

In fact, Dejaj Shehtou went as far north as Keren in the Bogos district, and Parkyns could not know that his expedition would start a dire chain of events for the Egyptians, the Abyssinians and the Baria. Together with the ravages committed by the raiding force in the Christian districts of Hamasien and Sarawa, Ras Oubie's operations in the winter of 1844 and 1845 stimulated friction and bloodshed that became a major factor in the affairs of northern Abyssinia. Later in the century, the unrest, personal rivalries and disloyalties created were a temptation to interfering Egyptian and Italian imperialists and culminated in the formation of the Italian colony of Eritrea in 1890.

While visiting the camp of Ras Oubie, both before and after the raid on the Baria, Parkyns was able to obtain and record a detailed account of the recent history of Tigré. After he had become familiar with the names of the leading participants, he listened with understanding to reminiscences and anecdotes from many sources, including men 'who were supposed to be good at relating stories of the last reign or so'. He kept his historical enthusiasms under control; he wrote:

> Of the earlier history of the country, as recorded in the ancient native chronicles, I do not attempt to give any account . . . I never saw the outside of the Kibir Za Negust, unless it were one of a pile of MSS which my friend Mr. A. D'Abbadie showed me . . .

No wonder modern historians have made little use of his book as an acknowledged source. His racy and amateurish style lacks academic respectability. Instead, it provides a story of anarchy that is intelligible only to a reader who is prepared to wrestle with its complexities, and it says much for Parkyns' intellectual gifts that he could record it as well as he did. Yet it has an authenticity that surpasses in some respects the accounts of modern historians who incline towards dressing up the Abyssinian characters of the period in the clothes of European statemanship. To write, for example, that 'Dejaj Wubie wrote to Queen Victoria' may be factual, and certainly it conveys a sense of serious participation in international affairs; but what was the reality?

Ras Oubie had never been outside his country and had probably never seen the sea. He had no 'chancellery' for dealing with foreign affairs and his perception of Queen Victoria was as uninformed as European perceptions of an Abyssinian ruler. This did not mean that he was ignorant of his own interests, or unable to contend with foreigners as realistically as he did with his rivals among his neighbouring rulers in Abyssinia.

When he addressed a letter to Queen Victoria or King Louis-Philippe, as he did on a few occasions, it was at the prompting of some English or French adventurer who hoped to attract advantage to himself, if only by inflating his own importance through meddling in the ruler's affairs. The letter itself was usually drafted by the adventurer and translated, or penned by an Ethiopic scribe on very general instructions from the ruler. When, months later, it reached the Foreign Office, or the Quai d'Orsay, rather than Buckingham Palace or the Tuileries, a scholar had to be found to translate it as best he could – not always correctly. The result would be read with amusement and an atlas would be consulted to establish the location of Abyssinia. Thereafter, thought would be given to disposing of the missive in a manner that would permit all concerned to turn to more important matters.

While Parkyns was at Adwa, Father de Jacobis and Wilhelm Schimper persuaded Ras Oubie to put his seal to a letter to King Louis-Philippe containing a half-baked request by Ras Oubie for 'French protection' against the Turks at Massawa. Presumably, they hoped that they themselves and the Lazarite mission would have the protection of the French Government from the British, in the person of William Coffin and the Church Missionary Society. When the letter reached Paris, François Guizot, then the French Foreign Minister, gave instructions to: 'Restrain the zeal of these gentlemen'. The matter lapsed.

In the 1840s coherent relations between the rulers of Abyssinia and the rest of the world had not yet been established and were to be long deferred, providing fertile ground for misunderstanding and misbehaviour. At the time, relations with Europe played a very minor part in the total activities of the rulers. Parkyns made no mention of them. When circumstances obliged the French and British governments, rather than individual French and British adventurers, to consider their attitudes to Abyssinia, they decided against involvement. The Magdala incident that brought a British expedition into the country temporarily, and the 'scramble for Africa', in its Abyssinian context spearheaded by Egypt, were decades ahead.

As for Parkyns' observations of 'manners and customs', he explained:

> I thought the wisest plan I could adopt was to domesticate myself as much as possible with the natives, the better to study their habits and modes of life. Although I had every opportunity for doing so, I did not exert myself as much as I might have done.

Parkyns was prepared to turn his hand to anything without a thought of the impression it made on others. For example, when he studied the silver ornaments worn by men and women at Adwa – buckles, anklets, bracelets, badges, etc. – he broadened his knowledge by working for the Greek silversmith

Michael whom he considered a thorough-paced rogue, and others of his craft. While doing so, he learnt much about how to debase the silver Michael used from melted coins:

> I have known a man to receive thirty Venetian sequins for a job, on which he employed only seven and a half. It is, perhaps, scarcely fair of me 'to tell tales out of school', for I was for a considerable time employed by them, and in consequence acquired a knowledge of many of their secret goings-on. But, in truth, they were more to be pitied than blamed. They are considered almost in the light of slaves here; that is, they are not allowed to leave the country; and though treated with considerable kindness, and even some distinction, their supplies are neither over-plentiful nor very regularly paid.

In his notes on domestic customs, Parkyns gave a perceptive account of matters that other travellers regarded as examples of savagery. One that attracted attention when he published *Life in Abyssinia* concerned the eating of raw meat:

> Raw meat, if kept a little time, gets tough; whereas, if eaten fresh and warm, it is far tenderer than the most tender joint that has been hung a week in England. The taste is, perhaps from imagination, rather disagreeable at first, but far otherwise when one gets used to it . . . When a cow is killed in a chieftain's establishment, there is not a part of it, from the horns to the hoofs, that does not belong by right to some member of the household. For instance, the gunners have the 'frimbia', a strip down the chest. The royal washerman has the 'tooncha', or second joint of one leg; while the shield-bearer has the similar joint on the other . . . The hump is the privilege of the great men only; the most renowned warrior among them has the first cut at it.

Claiming the first cut sometimes became a matter of serious dispute and he recalled the experience of a Tigrean warrior who was first to plunge his knife into a cow's hump at a feast attended by two Amhara braves of repute. The argument was so warm that 'He fought them both on horseback, and, what's more, killed them both'.

To this, Parkyns linked two important problems of personal relations:

[95]

Vanity is one of the principal besetting sins of the Abyssinians; and it is this weakness, when brought out by liquor, that is the origin of most of these quarrels . . . Words are bandied about without measure: insults follow; then blows . . . I have always found that the best plan for keeping a man quiet, when in this state, was to remark to him that it was unbecoming in a great man to behave in such a way – that people of rank were dignified and reserved in their manners and conversation. And thus I have argued very successfully . . .

At least half of *Life in Abyssinia*, which was published in two volumes, is devoted to 'manners and customs' in various forms. He dealt with clothing, cooking, brewing, domestic servants, musical instruments, births, marriages, deaths, funerals, nicknames, and the like. On religious matters, he confessed his lack of knowledge and drew on Samuel Gobat's book;* but he touched on aspects of the subject that had come to his notice by direct experience: fasts and feasts, the calendar, hagiology, sanctuary, Hebraic survivals, and the characteristics of priests, for example. Customs with a magical content interested him particularly: protection from the evil eye, belief in omens, charms, serpent cults and cures for lunacy.

In the field of necromancy also, he enlarged his knowledge by direct experience, particularly about the influence of local devils on his female retainers. 'It will be a rather long task', he wrote, 'to explain the workings of these malignant spirits, their nature and origin, and the mode of expulsion . . . having seen above a hundred cases of his work'. He described the activities of Bouda among others, who affected blacksmiths 'who are supposed to have the power of turning themselves into hyenas'.

Bouda could also 'possess' other victims, especially women: 'the reason of their being attacked is often that they have despised the proffered love of some Bouda, or for other similar cause'. For protection, children were given names in addition to their baptismal names – gold, silver, joy, sweetness, etc. – because:

a Bouda cannot act upon a person whose real name he does

---

* *Journal of a Three Years' Residence in Abyssinia in Furtherance of the Objects of the Church Missionary Society* (London, 1834).

not know . . . Should he however have obtained the true name of his victim, he takes a particular kind of straw, and, muttering something over it, bends it in a circle, and places it under a stone. The person thus doomed is taken ill at the very moment of the bending of the straw.

Naturally, the activities of Bouda also became involved in cases of hysteria and Parkyns went to extraordinary lengths to observe the symptoms. A brief example of one of his 'case histories' concerned a servant-girl in his house:

who sank into a state of lethargy, approaching to insensibility. Either from excellent acting and great fortitude, or from real want of feeling, the various experiments that we made on her seemed to have no more effect than they would have on a mesmeric somnambulist. We pinched her but she never moved a muscle of her face. I held a bottle of strong sal volatile under her nose, and stopped her mouth; but although I should wager any amount that she had never seen, smelt, or heard of such preparation as liquid ammonia, it had no more effect on her than rosewater . . . I had a charm which I usually wore for various maladies; but I am perfectly sure that one for the Bouda was not among them. Still, hoping thereby to expose the cheat, I asserted that there was a very celebrated one, and laid it on her face, expecting that she would pretend to feel the effects, and act accordingly; but, to my surprise and disappointment, she remained quite motionless. Several persons had been round the village to look for some talisman, but only one was found. On it being applied to her mouth she for an instant sprang up, bit at it, but then laughed, and said it was weak, and would not vex *him* . . .

Strange to say, that very night, for the first and last time that I ever heard him during my stay at Rohabeita, an hyena kept howling and laughing close to the village: consequently, his appearance that evening was hailed by all the people with a feeling of horror, as they doubtless connected it with the woman's sickness. I was regarded, even by my own servants, as a man devoid of all sensibility, because I ventured to smile at the idea, and to treat the whole matter as an imposture.

Eventually, the Bouda was smoked out of her by burning a concoction prescribed by Parkyns that consisted of:

two or three bits of dry bamboo-roots wrapped carefully in a piece of paper, together with an old leaf or two, some pipe-ashes, and a bit of hair which I cut off the tail of my faithful dog Maychal Boggo.

An instance of the application of more orthodox psychology occurred at Addi Abbo. The chief, Aito Merratch, had a mentally-deranged boy in his household: 'a poor fellow whom he took about with him as an occasional source of amusement'. Parkyns noticed 'that his paroxysms increased according to as he had been baited or laughed at by the men . . . So I begged Merratch to let me have him for a while, saying that I would try to cure him'. By protecting the boy from ridicule and giving him some pride in performing simple personal services for him, Parkyns made him 'quite steady and tolerably reasonable. When I returned him to Merratch, he insisted I had wrought this wonderful cure in him by means of medicine or charms'. A year later, the boy brought him 'a small present of bread, the produce of his own cultivation . . . and cried bitterly on my telling him that I was about to leave the country, and that he could not come with me'.

The chapter in *Life in Abyssinia* on 'Government Laws, Etc.' Parkyns wrote from memory because his papers, containing 'a good deal of information on these interesting subjects', were destroyed in crossing a river on his way out of the country:

> From their being of a nature not so easily remembered as ceremonies which one has witnessed, my memory and the few scanty notes which I retained have assisted me less perhaps than in any other part of the work, always excepting geography.

Nevertheless, he gave an adequate outline of the provincial jurisdictions into which the ancient kingdom had dissolved, of the powers of the provincial rulers and their administration of justice supported by anecdotes on trials he had witnessed, of oaths, punishments and the treatment of debtors, of taxation and military obligations.

A chapter headed 'Anecdotes Illustrative of Character, Etc.', he prefaced with the comment that:

> Travellers are apt to attribute to an entire population traits that have been observed in the townspeople, or even in their

own immediate followers ... There are errors, too, into which the readers of travels may fall as well as the writer; such as attributing to character what may belong only to custom; as, for instance, natural cruelty to a people on account of certain of their habits in war being cruel.

Most European travellers stressed the cruelty of Abyssinians to men and beasts: the punitive cutting off of hands and feet; the blindings; the flayings that men suffered; and the cutting of steaks from living cattle, a story that got James Bruce into much trouble.

Parkyns commented after his return to England:

I have heard it remarked that it was scarcely possible to believe human beings capable of such cruelty. In answer to this, I would merely observe that no one should venture on such a remark in a country where salmon are crimped, and eels skinned alive; nor should they talk of cruelty of any sort till the state trials and other books, showing the horrible death which many of our ancestors suffered for their adherence to the Stuart family, be out of print, and the old sentence for high treason forgotten.

One of his own Parkyns ancestors had suffered this dreadful penalty. In his opinion:

The Abyssinian has much kindly feeling, although in fight he considers his victory incomplete unless he horribly mutilates his fallen foe . . . We pick out some striking custom, and from it deduce the national character, forgetting that they would possibly remark something about us which would lead them to entertain precisely the same opinion of us as we had formed of them.

It was well that he made these comments because there followed a recital of atrocities. To readers who might ask why he had made insufficient mention of any of the people's good points:

I answer, simply because anecdotes of benevolence, justice, fidelity, etc., are rarely interesting enough to become topics of conversation . . . I shall only say that among the unsophisticated peasantry of Tigré there exists a full average proportion of good qualities.

The participants in nearly all the horrific stories he recorded were, he believed, either Amharas or Gallas.

> In general, I refer to the Amhara soldiers in Tigré, for I profess to knowing nothing about the Amhara peasantry at home . . . I hated the name of Amhara and never permitted the language to be used in my house . . . everything that one sees or hears of them in Tigré is of the worst description.

No doubt he echoed the assertions of his Tigrean acquaintances.

Throughout the year at Adwa there were holidays and saints' days which were usually the occasions for feasting, drinking and games, although they were far outnumbered by the days of fasting. Parkyns was more interested in the games than in the religious significance of these celebrations.

> Of all their feasts, that of Maskal, or the Cross, is the one which is celebrated with the greatest amount of pomp and outward show. During the whole of the interval between St. John's day and this feast a desultory warfare is carried on between the young people of the opposite sexes in the towns. They all sally out in the evenings, the girls armed with gourds containing a filthy solution . . . while the lads are provided with nettles or thistles as weapons of offence. When any of the hostile parties meet, the contest commences by the members of each sex insulting those of the other with the most obscene and offensive language. In this warfare the female tongue, as in all countries, has, of course, the advantage. Then the boys attack the girls . . . while the fair ones retaliate by discharged portions of their odoriferous compound in the faces of their assailants.

Parkyns himself joined in another traditional affray.

> At Adoua the different parishes have a regular fight, which put me strongly in mind of a Cambridge 'town and gown' row . . . The united parishes of St. Michael and St. Gabriel, beat and put to flight the men of St. Saviour's. I was of the retreating party . . . Beyond a few roughish club knocks, it is rarely that any serious consequences occur . . . I always made a point of entering into the spirit of the people on these

occasions, and I believe gained many friends by so doing.

These sporting parishes, Parkyns explained, also:

> play at 'hockey', in precisely the same manner as we do in England. At Adoua the goals are the churches of St. Michael and St. Gabriel, past which each party strives to drive the ball. They play with clubs with large heads and a wooden ball. When the game is ended the victorious party dance, and sing a sort of war-chant, 'Aho, oho, ahai, ahai, ahai'. All these scenes are very wild and interesting . . . Some of the dances are worth all the Giselles and Sylphides that ever appeared on the boards of an opera-house.

From the number of anecdotes he used to illustrate the points he made on manners and customs, he must have done a great deal of listening and questioning; but conversation was not his only diversion. He sometimes became involved in more formal contests and games:

> I have had many a friendly bout with the natives – a Turkish pipe-stick being my weapon, against a long bamboo and shield; and I have always come off victorious, never finding a man who could in any way touch me . . . They considered me a sort of Admirable Crichton in swordsmanship. It is true, I used to be celebrated, as a boy, at singlesticks, and have taken lessons in fencing of Coulon, at Paris. The Abyssinians never objected to have a bout with me for a jar of beer, knowing that the liquor was more frequently drunk by the vanquished than by the victor. A sword in the hand of an Abyssinian is almost useless, because he holds his shield before him with his left hand, and dares not to advance his right shoulder, lest he should uncover his body.

Not only did Parkyns join in the ceremonies and games, he was also recklessly willing to try anything he came across, tattooing, for instance:

> I had one arm adorned; a rather blind old woman was the artist; her implements consisted of a little pot of some blacking, and a large home-made iron pin . . . With some persons, the first effect of this tattooing is to produce a considerable amount of fever.

Apart from these informative Abyssinian contacts, his year at Adwa also brought him some new European acquaintances. Among them was Father de Jacobis, the Roman Catholic missionary whom Parkyns had first met on his way up from the coast. He must have seen more of him at Adwa than he admits in his journal, for he confided to Milnes, in a letter written from Adwa: 'Don't mention it, but I am now nearly, if not quite, a Catholic'.

It was his association with de Jacobis that led him into expressing his opinions about missionary activities in general, including some forthright assertions about the Protestant missionaries expelled from Tigré by Ras Oubie in 1839.

Parkyns never met a Protestant missionary although he heard plenty of opinions on them from his Abyssinian acquaintances. When he wrote his book some years later, he prefaced his remarks on the subject by reminding his readers that he was 'a mere lad' at the time and unqualified to judge their achievements. However, he found that the missionaries had left 'not one single convert, nor even one individual who would say more of them than they were good-natured open-handed people, and that it was a pity that they were such desperate heretics'. He understood that the orthodox Abyssinian Copts were 'naturally offended at the intrusion of persons whose avowed object was to uproot the religion they have received from their ancestors, and which is as dear and sacred to them as our one to us'.

It appears that he was impressed more by Father de Jacobis' personality than by his sanctity. The priest was of Neapolitan origin, and all who met him testified to his sympathetic and winning manner. His humility, we are told, made a deep impression on his Abyssinian acquaintances. Subsequently he took the initiative in creating a Roman Catholic Church of the Ethiopic rite to avoid offending too harshly the traditions of the indigenous Coptic Christians. Its churches and their congregations are still to be found in Eritrea. That de Jacobis was no less a person than Parkyns judged him to be, is borne out by his subsequent beatification. In Tigré he was involved, it must be said, in political activities of a kind that would have attracted criticism if associated with a less sanctified figure.

The person who gave Father de Jacobis advice and support was Dr Wilhelm Schimper, the German naturalist. De Jacobis converted him to Catholicism, but some wondered if Schimper had not taken the step in order to demonstrate his independence from the German Protestant missionaries, employed by the Church Missionary Society, who had been expelled from Tigré by Ras Oubie. In 1844, Schimper was given by Ras Oubie a fief of some small villages in the district of Antioch, a long day's march north-east of Adwa.

While Parkyns was living at Adwa he met a German sea captain called Albert Rödatz whose brig *Alph* called at Massawa while on a trading voyage in the Red Sea. Having read about Schimper's experiences, he determined to visit him, ostensibly with a view to raising money in Germany for carrying out Schimper's plans for the colonization of Tigré: another example of the effect of the altitude on the judgement of the European residents of Adwa. Rödatz's immediate purpose was to buy Abyssinian mules for export to Mauritius.

Captain Rödatz performed a useful service for Parkyns by carrying his letters and a bale of bird specimens to Captain Haines at Aden; but Parkyns remembered him best because he lent him a copy of Marryat's *Peter Simple*, the only English book he saw during his stay in Abyssinia. Unfortunately his tame monkey tore it into shreds before he had finished it. Of Parkyns, Captain Rödatz wrote:

> He is a refined Englishman; a traveller who, after roaming through the continent and Egypt has arrived in Abyssinia . . . If one seeks in Mr. Parkyns' appearance the elegantly cultivated and pampered European, one would search in vain. He is wholly Abyssinian, he goes half-naked without covering to his head or feet. His earlier rather pale complexion is deeply sunburnt, and in his deportment and movement he cannot be distinguished from the Abyssinians, although in dealing with Europeans, the well-informed, cultivated Englishman shines forth . . . The greater part of the six days I stayed in Adwa I passed with Mr. Parkyns. We rode and went together; hunted and gossiped the rest of the time.

Parkyns' other European visitor was the Franco-Irish explorer, Antoine d'Abbadie, who passed through Adwa in September 1844 on his way to Massawa, but it was not until two years later that he mentioned his meeting with Mansfield

Parkyns at Adwa in a letter to the editor of *The Athenaeum*. 'The week I spent with him', he wrote, 'is one of my happiest recollections of Abyssinia'.

When Captain Rödatz, in his brig *Alph* returned to Aden, he told Captain Haines of Parkyns' difficulties. Shortly afterwards, his letters and newspapers, accidentally delayed *en route*, arrived in Aden together with two boxes of things he had ordered. In May 1845, Haines sent them to Massawa, together with some money on account, in the Indian Navy's schooner *Constance* used for collecting intelligence about what was afoot on the Red Sea and East African coasts. Parkyns had news of them in advance and all was excitement when they arrived at Adwa. 'I realized', Parkyns wrote, 'a pleasure in reading letters and newspapers which I had by no means expected, my ideas and feelings having become rather Abyssinian.'

Among the letters was one from his solicitor in Nottingham urging him to execute a power of attorney in favour of his brother. If Parkyns had been mystified by not receiving any communications from England, his family were no less perplexed by not hearing from him, and had decided that he was probably dead. However, if he were alive, he had now come of age and had inherited the manor of East Leake on the Leicestershire border. Also one of his mother's family – George Smith – had died and left him a legacy. So he did as his solicitor wished and returned the power of attorney, duly witnessed by 'Michael the silversmith' and 'Dimitri the tailor', residents of Adwa. The document survived the long journey back to Nottingham where it remains a curiosity among his solicitor's papers.

Now that he was in funds once more and feeling in touch with home, Parkyns had to do some serious thinking. Shortly before, suspecting that he might have to stay in Tigré longer than he had anticipated, he discussed with Dejaj Lemma, Ras Oubie's senior son, the possibility of his taking the fief of Rohabeita, the frontier parish where he had spent the previous year. In return he would pay tribute and undertake 'to keep in order the hostile Barea, without putting Dejaj Lemma to any inconvenience on their score'; but Lemma had to obtain his father's approval, and there was delay. In the meantime, rumours of what was afoot leaked out and, as a result, 'many of those who had fled to distant provinces came, bringing me presents, and anxiously inquiring when they should be able to return to their former homes'.

With the arrival of money and supplies, he had no longer a valid excuse for remaining in Abyssinia:

> The rains were just setting in; still I felt that I must make up my mind for a start, or wait for another remittance; for, after my debts of honour, and the still more numerous and equally imperative debts of gratitude, were discharged, the balance would barely carry me to Sennar (on the Nile) . . . Accordingly I set about my preparations *instanter* . . . I will spare myself the recollection, and my readers the perusal, of a very moist, unpleasant leave-taking: a crowd of both sexes came to see me off, although to avoid such an occurrence I had secretly fixed my departure for an early hour in the morning . . . I believe that for the first time since my arrival in the country I wished I had had a pocket-handkerchief.

Dejaj Shehtou expressed his feelings for him by presenting him with his favourite horse.

His diary makes no reference to his temporary wife, Tures, nor to his son John who, according to family tradition at Adwa, was born to her. The relevant pages of his diary are missing.

Ninety-four years later, in April 1941, I called at Adwa during General Platt's invasion from the Sudan of Mussolini's Abyssinian empire, and met an assembly of notables in the town. When exchanges flagged, I thought I might revive them by asking whether anyone present had heard of the name of Mansfield Parkyns. It was soon evident that his name was not only remembered but remembered with respect, and information on the whereabouts of his great-grandson was volunteered. Subsequent inquiries left me in no doubt that the impression given in his diary of his happy relations with the people was in no way exaggerated. On the other hand, European visitors during the last century whom one might expect to be better remembered, had been forgotten altogether.

8

Of the half-dozen explorers of the period who arrived in Abyssinia with vaguely expressed intentions of crossing the continent to the Atlantic, only Mansfield Parkyns made a determined attempt to continue his journey to the west beyond the Abyssinian highlands. According to Antoine d'Abbadie when he met Parkyns at Adwa, his former companions, John Bell and Walter Plowden, had still not advanced beyond Begemder. Bell had become one of Ras Ali's retainers, and Plowden had been visiting a Wollo chieftain.

When he left Adwa in June 1845, Parkyns decided to take the direct route to Khartoum, at the junction of the Blue and White Niles, instead of following the beaten track of the caravans to Gondar; and then on to Metemma, Sennar and Khartoum. The direct route was shorter but still covered some 500 miles. Following it entailed particular difficulties during the rainy season because of the many rivers to be crossed between Adwa and the frontier with the Sudan. However, he was attracted by the possibility this route offered for his visiting Mek Nimr, a Sudanese leader of the Ja'alin tribe; a name familiar to all Europeans who read about this part of Africa. They understood that *Mek* meant 'King', and *Nimr* meant 'Leopard', and that he had defied the Pasha of Egypt. Indeed, he had caused the Pasha's son to be burned to death. No European, and certainly no Egyptian, had ever visited his refuge on the fringes of the Abyssinian highlands.

On leaving Adwa, Parkyns made for Walkait, a province north of Gondar, beyond which were the cotton-soil plains of the eastern Sudan, heavy mud and malarial pools after falls of rain. He felt equal to the challenge, for, by this time, he had a well-organized train of followers, and he was fully accustomed to Abyssinian travel. As a personal servant, the jet black Sa'id, who was lapsing increasingly into drunkenness, recruited a local man at Adwa who, like himself, had previously worked for the French staff officers, Ferret and Galinier. Gabre Mariam continued in Parkyns' service until he died some years later at Ruddington, near Nottingham, as tenant of Abyssinia Cottage, opposite the church.

Before Parkyns left, Wilhelm Schimper asked him to take with him a German deserter from Captain Rödatz's ship at Massawa, who according to Parkyns, arrived at Adwa expecting great things 'having heard that Mr. Schimper was a prince'. He had hoped to find employment with his countryman, being a man who could turn his hand to anything. Parkyns warned him that the journey to Khartoum 'would not perhaps be the most agreeable one, except for the novelty and adventure it might afford . . . but he declared that he should much prefer my route, and, as for roughing it, the more of that the merrier'. Parkyns never obtained his real name, but he was known as Yacoub, the Arabic version of Jacob.

That Parkyns began his journey at a time when the rainy season was setting in, is the measure of his impulsiveness. The main obstacle ahead was the River Takazze which was rising daily and it was important that the party should cross it without delay. Unfortunately, on the day after he left Adwa, he began to suffer from inflammation of his eyes; presumably a form of conjunctivitis. With his eyes bandaged, the party travelled over familiar ground; towards the monastery of Debra Abai, built in a cleft in the escarpment on the north side of the Takazze river. Had he been able to see it, he might have admired the awe-inspiring mountains beyond the river, to the south.

At Debra Mai, he was delayed by his eye infection which obliged him to stay in the dark inside the guest-room of the monastery. Conjunctivitis is an unpleasant complaint, described by Parkyns as: 'the agreeable sensation of having your eyes filled with sharp, coarse sand, red hot'. For its treatment he 'ate next to nothing, took plenty of jalop, etc., had some blood taken from behind the ears, and a few drops of solution of sulphate of zinc dropped into each eye three or four times a day'. Yacoub, the German, nursed him 'most tenderly', and gradually he regained his sight.

The country before them was known to be difficult and it was important that the party should cross the swollen Takazze while they could. So they obtained a guide at the monastery and left as soon as Parkyns was fit to travel. They descended some thousands of feet to the river through a jumble of gullies and ravines, and through scrub that turned into large trees on the river's banks. Most of the party ran ahead to the water. Parkyns recalled:

> Some of our people had never seen a river of any sort, and looked upon it with awe and wonder. Indeed, it was a noble stream, in many places nearly, if not quite, as broad as the Thames at Greenwich; but in its rapid, boisterous descent, more like the Rhone as it leaves the Lake of Geneva.

The guide led the party downstream to a point at which he judged it safe to cross. Perishables were packed in skins and all was made ready: 'We began to strip, and tie up our clothes in bundles, which we were to carry, each man his own, turban-like, on his head'. Yacoub, the German, waded out into the water and he exchanged gleeful shouts with Parkyns.

> I did not think there could be any danger, and he had told me that he was an extremely good swimmer . . . I again called to him and he answered something that made me laugh, at the same time swinging his arms about like the sails of a windmill, so as to splash the water all around him.

A moment later the German was being swirled along uncontrollably in the flood. Parkyns raced along the bank but, while avoiding a thicket of canes and bushes, he lost sight of the river and the helpless Yacoub.

> Before I reached the other end of them the horrible death-howl of the Abyssinians warned me that he had sunk to rise

no more. We ran along the shore in the melancholy hope that perhaps the torrent might cast his body on to some bank, but it was an almost hopeless chance.

On the following morning the river was higher, but the party managed to cross it without further accident. They were all depressed and disheartened at the suddenness of the cheerful German's disappearance.

I doubt if any of us slept soundly; for my part I started up twice, once fancying that I heard the death-howl again, and once that poor Yakoub was calling me by name . . . I must say for the Abyssinians and blacks also that they manifested much sympathy and kindness of heart, appearing to feel as deeply for our poor friend's fate as if he had been a near relation to them, although he had only been with us a few days, and, except by signs and a few broken words, he could converse with none of the party.

Yacoub was not the only loss Parkyns sustained during this crossing of the Takazze, and his discovery that his personal talisman was missing came as a shock. He had worn it round his neck in a small leather satchel during the whole of his stay in Abyssinia, and he had become convinced that it was in some way responsible for his good luck and good health since his arrival in the country. The talisman, which he told Abyssinian inquirers to be a relic of a saint, was, in fact, the remains of the flowery buttonhole he had found among his effects in Cairo:

My withered flowers had a charm for me, besides that of superstition . . . for they formed the last link that connected me with the life I had been brought up to. At times, when lost in the excitement of a savage life and dazzled by the splendour of a tropical climate, they would remind me of friends and scenes I had left behind; paint civilization in her brightest colours, and even so far 'humbug' me as to persuade me that a drizzly November day was only a foil to set off the brightness of an English fireside.

After their unhappy crossing of the Takazze river, Parkyns and his party found themselves in the district of Walda-Ab; a wild place known for its monasteries, its religious zealots, and its exposure to raids by the Baria and Baza tribes. Human skulls and bones by the wayside were attributed to them. The travellers were now marching parallel to the Takazze and to the south of it, so that they had to cross the streams tumbling down from the mountains after each daily rainstorm; some of them considerable torrents, particularly the Zarima which delayed them for four days while they waited for the level of its water to fall.

In the meantime, they ran out of food. 'We had only a very few dried vetches each for food, and were miserably off in other respects, for the rain poured down on us three hours out of every four.' The more resourceful members of the party caught and devoured 'any newt, lizard, snake, or other reptile they might chance to meet with'. Their hardships were a stimulus to action. 'Four days of this sort of life being enough for us, we determined to try and swim the river.' First, the guide crossed with another good swimmer, but the river, although not wide, poured through a rocky gully and carried anyone crossing it far downstream. So the guide returned and made what he claimed to be a raft, although Parkyns thought it resembled

> such a bundle as an old woman would carry under her arm from a hedge-bottom. I tried its buoyance in a backwater, and laughed heartily at its maker on finding that it could not even float itself, much less carry me . . . 'And is this the bark which is to carry Caesar and his fortunes?' . . . We dropped into the stream, and away we went.

It was a desperate venture. A few of the Abyssinians in the party refused to cross and turned back. A mule was swept away with its load, including some of Parkyns' papers and diary.

They had no choice but to press on in search of food, although this meant the crossing of more torrents in a state of flood that would normally have been regarded as too dangerous for swimmers. The villages in the vicinity were on the summits of hills, for protection from Baria raiders.

At last they saw a more accessible settlement above them:

> It was near sunset when we arrived, and, shortly after, a peasant with a flock of goats passed on his way homeward. Seeing that we were half starved, he endeavoured to drive a very hard bargain with us, but at last we induced him to sell us a little milk and an old he-goat for twice its value.

They then ate him all but raw, and the repast gave Parkyns indigestion for days to come.

On the following day, they made a long and rough descent from this elevated village, during which the horse given him by Dejaj Shehtou, while walking alone behind Parkyns, 'performed a complete summersault, from the top of a rock into a mass of bushes below, with no more misfortune than the breakage of his saddle'. However, it spilled the contents of his saddle-bag and although his servants collected most of them, his journal and scientific observations, together with some sketches, were missing when he checked his possessions later.

There was nothing for it but to march on over more low-lying muddy country to the next range of high hills, on which was the town of Kafta, the market to which merchants from the Sudan – Arabs to the Abyssinians – came to exchange salt from the Red Sea for Abyssinian cotton stuffs and slaves. Kafta marked a new stage in his progress to the west, but it also presented new difficulties.

The frontier between Abyssinia and the Sudan is a natural as well as a political one since it marks broadly the limit of the Abyssinian highlands and the plain of the Nilotic Sudan. In 1845 it was undefined and troublesome and it was not formally delimited until some sixty years later. Along it were scattered settlements of Muslim pilgrims from countries west of the Nile, people who had embarked on the years-long pilgrimage to Mecca but who had decided not to return home. On the frontier, they occupied Tom Tiddler's ground, endeavouring to evade the jurisdiction either of the Turko-Egyptian authorities, or of the Abyssinians.

Not far west of Kafta was the other settlement Parkyns was determined to visit, made up of fugitives from the Nile north of Khartoum. This was the refuge of Mek Nimr who had caused the death, twenty years earlier of Ismail, the son of Muhammed Ali Pasha of Egypt. Mek Nimr led a precarious existence between the Egyptians, who wanted to capture and execute him, and the Abyssinians who were not reluctant to have Mek Nimr and his people between themselves and their Muslim neighbours.

The problems this insecure frontier presented to a visiting European were soon made clear to Parkyns. In Tigré he was usually designated a Copt; now he was accused of being a Turk and wherever he asked for lodging at Kafta he received a direct refusal until by

the use of every means of persuasion I could command, I got leave from a very poor man to occupy a wretched hovel adjoining his habitation. Here I determined on a quiet halt for a few days, as I and most of my servants had been more or less ailing ever since we had eaten the old he-goat.

On the third night a party of soldiers came to arrest him and take him before Lij Hailu, the local Abyssinian authority. His arrest was rough although he added to his account of it: 'I was wrong in saying the soldiers were rough; it was only their leader Bellata Wassan, an ugly old brute, who began to bully and bluster'. And so he was brought before Lij Hailu feeling ill and in a bad temper, demanding to be told the reason for his treatment. 'A little more sparring of this sort ensued . . . and it ended in my being consigned to a squad of soldiers, with orders that I was not to leave their hut on any pretext'.

He was still suspected of being a Turkish spy despite his assertions that he had come from Adwa and that he was the friend of Dejaj Shehtou. Happily his prison turned out to be a good deal more commodious than his previous shelter and the soldiers gave him a bed to lie on.

I soon slept off my troubles. Next day I awoke quite in my usual state of philosophy and highly amused at my situation. After some little 'chaffing', of which I took no notice, the soldiers began to dance about, going through their war-boast, and coming up to me, slipping lances at me, and catching them by the butt when the point was within an inch or two of my body. I knew very well I was in no danger if I only kept my temper, so when the first man had performed his part, I took a piece of straw and gave it to him, telling him that it was a sword which I saw he needed; this raised a laugh against him, and, entering into the spirit of the thing, we went on famously – I acted the part of chief . . . while, to make the matter appear more real (as Mr. Swiveller remarked to the Marchioness), I invested a dollar (which I luckily had tied up in the corner of my belt) in some mead and we had a mock feast. Thus we passed a whole afternoon in a most agreeable manner, and I became a great favourite with the soldiery, instead of being bullied by them . . . Let this be a warning to hot-headed travellers.

Fortunately, his servants had heard that a chieftain senior to Lij Hailu had encamped two days away and they went to him with the story that Parkyns had been sent to the Sudan by Dejaj Shehtou to procure firearms for him. The story was an invention, but one of the chief's retainers remembered having seen Parkyns in Dejaj Shehtou's company at Adwa and it was decided that Parkyns should be freed. At once the atmosphere around him changed. Lij Haliu asked him to dinner and presented him with a carved wooden back-scratcher. Presents of food were brought, together with 'a buffoon to cheer my evening and a singing woman of great beauty and considerable talent'. Despite the change in atmosphere he decided on the following morning to move on without further delay.

During his stay at Kafta, Parkyns met two young men who were hostages, or rather sureties for the payment of dues to Lij Hailu; Abu Bakr, one of Mek Nimr's sons, and Abu Rejjab, the chief of one of the West African villages. They were valuable acquaintances who assured Parkyns of a friendly welcome when he arrived at Mai Gubba, Mek Nimr's village situated at a lower level west of Kafta, although well elevated above the plain for protection against raiding Egyptian troops. From it there was a wide view over the valleys leading to the plains of the Sudan, a sparsley populated country covered with long grass and open bush.

At Mai Gubba, Parkyns went to call on Mek Nimr's eldest surviving son, called Omar – in Parkyns' phonetic spelling it became Imr – who, since his aged father was blind, was the effective leader of these Ja'alin fugitives from the Nile. But the Ja'alin were now in the minority at Mai Gubba, for the settlement had attracted many others who wished to avoid the Egyptian authorities. According to Parkyns: 'They were a mixture of runaway slaves, deserters from the black regiments in the Egyptian service, and escaped malefactors of all sorts'.

He was charmed by Imr's Sudanese hospitality and friendly manners. He and his party had travelled all day in a deluge of rain and they were cold, wet, and tired. The hut to which they were shown had a warm fire: 'even the Abyssinian servant who accompanied me acknowledged that this was better than in his own country'. Imr welcomed them cordially and politely, and talked with them for some time. Parkyns' colloquial Arabic was by now pretty fluent, if broad in accent, from his practising the language with his servants and Arabic-speaking visitors to Adwa. Imr invited them to stay a few days and, after drinking coffee and tasting some grilled bones, he left. Before long a beautiful slave girl, clad only in

> a fringe of thin leather shreds worn round the loins, the whole indoor costume of an unmarried girl in Nubia, arrived with a bowl of new milk . . . It was nectar! and the bearer was Hebe! But no juice of the treacherous vine was ever half as sweet as that milk.

Glowing with the first nourishing meal he had eaten for some time, Parkyns was then taken to call on the old Mek Nimr, whose hut was only a few hundred yards away:

> We found him seated on a mat near the entrance, twiddling a rosary for a *passetemps*. I was disappointed in his appearance: judging from all I had heard of his deeds and character, I expected a physiognomy something like that of the repentant gentleman in Paradise and the Peri.

But Nimr was not at all like that:

> Murderer, outlaw, as he is called, and brigand (as I suspect he frequently is, after an honourable fashion), 'the Leopard' appeared to us in the shape of a good-natured looking old granddad, with a bald pate and comfortable rotundity. He is little darker than an Egyptian, and has a most benevolent expression of countenance, over which, however, one may occasionally detect the passage of a cloud . . . The poor old chief seemed to feel deeply the false character he bore among people who were unacquainted with him . . . He seemed quite pleased that I had come to see him, and once or twice said, 'You'll tell the world that after all you did not find us so very bad as some men think' . . . Imr afterwards asked me to use any influence I might gain among the Turkish authorities at Khartoum or in Egypt in procuring for them a paper of 'aman', or protection.

Parkyns was the only European to visit Mek Nimr at his refuge at Mai Gubba in the thirty years he lived there, and it was his first introduction to the Arabs of the Sudan; a people as agreeable and likable to him as they have been to many other Englishmen. For example, there was El Tayib, Mek Nimr's scribe with a particular gift for writing charms. When all Parkyns' animals strayed from their pasture, he thought they had been stolen. But El Tayib wrote him

> a powerful charm, which he assured me would not only protect them from all harm, but also lead them back to us by morning . . . so I sat down and talked with him on general subjects till supper time . . . We sat for a long time, and formed many grand plans for expeditions against the neighbouring tribes; for fortifying the hill on which the village stood, and thus rendering it a place of refuge for the villages of the plain; and a variety of other castles in the air'.

Imr joined in and they discussed a scheme by which Parkyns would become chief of the marauding Baza tribe, 'for by proper diplomacy I could have obtained the support of the Abyssinians on the one side and the Turko-Egyptian government on the other'.

Ten years later when he reverted, while farming in Nottinghamshire, to the entries in his journal for this period, he commented:

> Well, all these visions of dominion have ended in my being monarch of a very limited number of quadrupeds, and as for glory! I get occasionally upset into a manure heap by an unruly bull-calf, without even the local papers taking any notice of it. *Sic transit gloria mundi!*

Mek Nimr belonged to the family of the chiefs of the Ja'alin tribe of Arabian descent that had settled on the Nile north of Khartoum, having previously been nomads. In the previous century, he had been involved in tribal and family feuds, as the Ja'alin adopted a more settled form of life. He maintained his position and Shendi, where he lived on the eastern bank of the Nile, became an important market. There he entertained an envoy from Muhammed Ali Pasha of Egypt in 1813; a visit that marked the beginning of the Pasha's plan for the occupation of the Sudan. In 1820, the Pasha invaded. Mek Nimr put up no resistance and swore allegiance to the Sultan of Turkey before the commander of the Egyptian expeditionary force in the person of Muhammed Ali Pasha's young son Ismail. Nevertheless, he was required to accompany the Egyptian expedition to Sennar, the capital of the defeated Fung rulers of the Sudan, as a hostage, with the prospect of being impaled if the Ja'alin did anything to threaten the Pasha's authority. He survived.

Two years later, Ismail Pasha, who had been appointed governor-general of the newly conquered province, arrived once more at Shendi, on his way back to Cairo; he was ill and disappointed. Instead of obtaining 40,000 slaves for his father's army, as he was expected to do, he had captured only a third of that number. On his arrival at the town with a small escort, a long way ahead of his main force, he made extravagant demands on Mek Nimr for camels, horses, money and food, estimated to amount to the equivalent of £20,000. During the wrangle that ensued, Ismail struck Mek Nimr, then aged forty, with the stem of his Turkish pipe, and, during the night, the Mek took his revenge by piling wood around the Pasha's straw rest-house and burning him, and most of his entourage, to death. Those who tried to escape were cut down. The story appealed strongly to Europeans, as well as Sudanese, for incendiarism is always sensational.

As for Mek Nimr, he had to beat a hasty retreat to this distant part of the country; to the undefined frontier with Abyssinia. On the way he suffered defeat in a pitched battle, and his Sudanese rivals took the opportunity to harry his tribesmen, but once the fugitives were across the Atbara river they were comparatively safe. For twenty years before Parkyns had visited him, Mek Nimr had managed to avoid capture, even though his head would have been the highest prized trophy that could be sent to Muhammed Ali Pasha.

Mek Nimr died not long after Parkyns saw him at Mai Gubba, but Parkyns' friend Imr survived for a further fifteen years, until he died of wounds received in a brush with a force led by Musa Hamdi Pasha, a Turk who also befriended Parkyns. The rest of the fugitives at Mai Gubba were then allowed to return to their original home. They had never been a serious threat to the government in Khartoum, but for many years they had symbolized resistance to the Turks, an emotion that was to find violent expression another twenty years later under the Mahdi's leadership.

Parkyns' strayed animals responded to El Tayib's charm, for the lost mules were found on the following morning, grazing within a few hundred yards of the village. 'I only relate the facts as they occurred,' Parkyns commented, 'without hazarding an opinion on the subject.' The horse Dejaj Shehtou had given him when he left Adwa was in wretched condition as the result of the rough march, and he decided to leave him with 'Imr as a present. Later he had the satisfaction of hearing that the animal became a great favourite.

At length, they set out on a Monday; a lucky day for beginning a journey. 'Imr gave him camels, a guide, a sword and an amulet to protect him from the dangers of travel in a wild country. But Parkyns absolutely refused to accept a shirt of chain-mail that was pressed on him. And so he set off down the slopes to the valleys below, leaving behind him a reputation that survived the fourteen years that elapsed before Samuel Baker visited the same area. His assurances that he knew Parkyns was a sufficient passport for him to be treated as a privileged guest.

Below Mek Nimr's village on the hill was a settlement of some two thousands of his followers, or rather fugitives from the Sudan who wanted to be positioned so that they could escape across the Abyssinian frontier and into the hills if the authorities in the Sudan wanted to arrest them. 'I never saw a more ill-looking set of followers', Parkyns wrote:

A wretched old black faky (or priest) had the coolness to remark that I was a spy, and that it was imprudent to let me go. The guide answered that I was not a Turk, but a Christian Frank, coming from their friends the Abyssinians, and recommended by them . . . The Arabs argued that the person of a man who had eaten and lodged with their chief was sacred to them – the blacks, that a spy and Christian ought to be safe nowhere.

Eventually Mek Nimr's men prevailed, and Parkyns was allowed to pass.

The country was undulating and covered with thorn bush,

sparsely populated and alive with game of all kinds. However he was no longer interested in shooting, except for the pot. Only the giraffes he saw caused him to comment that their:

> long necks, acting as observatories, gave them due notice of our coming. Their gait is the most awkward looking of any animal that I know, being something between the up and down movement of a rocking horse and the waddle of a Greenwich pensioner on two wooden legs; nevertheless, they get over the ground at a great pace.

They were marching between two rivers coming from the Abyssinian highlands, mountains that receded daily behind them, to Parkyns' regret, as they advanced west. On their right was the Settit river, the local name for the Takazze of Abyssinia that Parkyns knew so well. On their left was the River Atbara into which the Settit and other tributaries collect before the main stream joins the Nile 260 miles to the north-west.

Consequently, they had no major river crossings to make until they reached the Ataba at Soufi. It turned out to be a strong and wide river with herds of elephants in the vicinity, but nothing like the mountain torrents they had faced in Walda-Ab. So they crossed it without mishap, with the help of inflated goatskins, to be met on the other bank by: 'a number of respectable and well-dressed gentlemen, who seemed as if they had known me before, they were so very civil and glad to see me.' To some extent, their affability reflected their hopes that the European might have property on which they could levy dues; but Parkyns had not much difficulty in disappointing them, although they thought that, at least, he ought to pay duty on one of his black servants as a slave. Parkyns explained that the man was, in fact, a Muslim pilgrim, and this satisfied them. 'After all,' he added, 'they *were* very good fellows; one of them had some first-rate tobacco, and allowed me to empty his bag into mine, asking only for a little honey, of which I had two large skins full.'

The party stayed three days at Soufi and Parkyns was struck by the glowing terms with which his hosts spoke of the Turko-Egyptian Government which he had been led to believe was generally detested, but he concluded, after further experience, that he was not sufficiently in their confidence for them to tell me their true feelings on the subject. There are too many spies about for an Arab to tell his opinion of the Turkish government to a stranger. I found this out some time after, by observing that a native's praise of his rulers generally diminished in proportion to the increase of our intimacy. For instance, many a man who, at our first interview, had spoken in the most glowing terms of the Turks in general and of his immediate governors in particular, has gradually come round, till, after some acquaintance, he would remark that they were the very scourge of the Almighty or of the devil . . . Such is, I believe, the true esteem in which they are mostly held by their southern subjects, and, I fear, is a pretty just one.

The country had become flat, an unending plain of black cotton-soil that was muddy and treacherous from the rain. The lack of geographical features made a traveller fresh from the scenery of Abyssinia feel rather lost and bored. For Parkyns, it was the reality of transcontinental African travel.

However, the boredom of the journey was alleviated by a Ja'alin tribesman who had joined them at Soufi.

Ali . . . succeeded in keeping is in a roar of laughter all the way by telling us stories, singing songs, and cracking jokes on everyone we passed . . . seriously confiding to them that I was a great Turk, travelling *incog.* by order of his highness Muhammed Ali Pasha, to see and report to him the conduct of the various governors, especially in regard to the treatment of his black subjects. I was immediately surrounded, everyone had some petition which I was to remember or some grievance which I was to lay before the Viceroy. It was of no use that I protested that I was nothing but a poor dervish.

The Blue Nile was still eight or nine days away, and to this Parkyns added a few days stay at the market of El Gedaref while he purchased two additional camels.

The market was a disappointment, although Parkyns had various experiences in the place that taught him more about the Sudan. A fierce-looking man accosted him and ordered him to follow, telling Parkyns' men to stay where they were. 'I asked him what he wanted. "Never you mind, only come along!", was his rather unsatisfactory reply.' At the far end of the village, he was dragged through a low door:

> The hut was partly lighted by a piece of rag, aided by a little fat in a clay saucer; around it sat a dozen or more half-naked armed savages. My guide led me across the apartment, and, taking a gourd full of some muddy-looking fluid from under a cloth, ordered me to drink. Was it deadly poison?

Far from it. It was *merissa*, the beer of the Sudan made from *sorghum*, the cereal of the northern Sudan; a beverage that is consumed in great quantities. 'I drank a good deal of it,' Parkyns explained, 'and then we had another supply, and another, until we got very affectionate . . . After a couple of hours passed in conviviality, I returned to my couch comfortably drowsy, and soon fell asleep.' It had been a perplexing introduction to social life in the Sudan at a level not usually experienced by visiting Europeans. He never met the Turkish officer of the area. Nor did it occur to him that he should 'collect' his acquaintance for reasons of prestige. He realized that his appearance might attract unwanted attention, for he explained:

> I was dressed in a pair of drawers, and a 'ferda' thrown over my shoulders. The heavy two-edged sword that 'Imr had given me hung over my left arm, to which also were bound a heap of amulets and a knife; so that in dress and weapons I was a nigger; in colour a Turk – an incongruity which probably never was seen in the Soudan before that day, nor perhaps ever will be again.

Already he was short of money, for, as usual, his expenditure had been too generous. And everyone in the party, apart from himself, was suffering from malaria. The rain poured down on them periodically, bringing with it the usual problems in crossing muddy depressions and watercourses with the attendant problem of keeping their scanty clothing dry. Parkyns' plan was simplicity itself:

> If halting, we took off our clothes and sat on them; if riding, they were placed under the leather shabraque of the mule's saddle, or under any article of similar material, bed or bag, that lay on the camel's back. A good shower-bath did none of

us any harm; and as soon as the rain was over, and the moisture on our skins had evaporated, we had our garments as warm, dry, and comfortable, as if they had been before a fire. In populous districts, we kept on our drawers, or supplied their place with a piece of rag, or a skin; and then, when the rain was over we wrapped ourselves up and taking off the wetted articles, hung them over the animals' cruppers to dry.

At length they reached the Blue Nile at a point just north of the river Rahad's junction with it, at a small town called Abu Heraz, where travellers could take boat down the Blue Nile to Khartoum; some ninety miles away. Abu Heraz could boast a few mud-brick houses and a small white-washed mosque. Parkyns wrote:

It was highly amusing to hear the remarks and speculations made on my appearance, especially when we passed the coffee-houses, where a number of Turkish soldiers were collected; my costume was certainly a queer one for a white man, and I determined to change it as soon as possible.

This was not easy but an Albanian irregular soldier told him that the clothes of one of his colleagues who had died of dysentery were about to be auctioned, and Parkyns was able to buy them for six and ninepence.

It took a few days to find a boat that would carry them to Khartoum; not a long journey with the river in flood. The animals he sent by land with Sa'id and two of the West Africans, but Ali and his Abyssinian servant Gabre Mariam embarked with him, in company with two Egyptian soldiers, a leprous Turk and two Greeks. One of the Greeks was a merchant with 'a formidable pair of moustachios'. Naturally he was known as Abu Shannab – he of the moustaches – and he enlivened the party on the boat with his stories:

. . . having in his memory a whole library of unpublished Arabic novels, after the style of the Thousand and One Nights, so that our crew, passengers and all, formed a circle round him every evening for an hour or two, and thus merrily passed the two days that we remained on board.

Khartoum, at the junction of the Blue and White Niles, had

been created some twenty years earlier as the Sudan's main administrative centre. Parkyns' companions had raised his expectations of what he would find there:

> Visions of the Golden Horn at Constantinople passed through my mind, and I own that I was a little disappointed . . . The suburbs which we first entered were transversed by alleys little more than a yard wide, the huts being half built of mud and decidedly inferior in architectural design to those constructed of the same material by a species of wasps in these countries . . . I held my tongue as long as I could not wishing to show my impatience; but when we came to nothing but a large open space of sandy ground, I could no longer refrain from asking, 'How much further is Khartoum?' 'Khartoum?' said my guide in accents of horror at my want of appreciation of the magnificence around me, 'Why, *this* is Khartoum; there before us is the palace of Moussa Bey', pointing to a long, low mud wall, with an unpainted doorway and a few unglazed windows.

Palaces were not for Parkyns. One of the Greeks in the boat 'good-naturedly offered to lodge me till I could find a place of my own, a piece of hospitality which of course, in the fulness of my heart and emptyness of my pocket, I thankfully accepted'. The accommodation was indifferent; a mud-brick room flanking the entrance to a compound; a room which Parkyns described as a 'gin-shop'.

> During the whole of every day, and the greater part of the night, the room was filled with Turks and Albanians, Greeks and Egyptians, blacks and mulattoes, who got drunk, fought, played cards and backgammon, sang songs, and amused themselves with the dancing girls in a most unseemly manner. Here I lodged; a bench covered with a mattress was my sleeping place, and also that of my Greek friend, and myriads of animalcula, *every* night, with the occasional addition of one or two of the customers who had been too drunk to go home.

This was urban life indeed.

Mentally depressed and physically weary, without his talisman to sustain him, Parkyns soon became the victim of the tropical disease he had so far, almost miraculously, avoided.

9

Parkyns was obliged to make radical adjustments in the Muslim Sudan to the way of life he had adopted in Christian Abyssinia. The climate was always more exacting than the one he had enjoyed in the Abyssinian highlands, and, for a European, often deadly.

When he first arrived in Khartoum, the room in which his friend Youssef Panajotti invited him to stay was rented by the Greek from the occupant of the compound beyond it. This contained a house belonging to a deceased French trader – Joseph Vaissiere – a Napoleonic veteran who fought with the Egyptian army in Arabia and who had later concerned himself with the slave trade in the Sudan. When Parkyns lodged at its entrance, the house was occupied by a Syrian – Ibrahim Kabir – who, having married Vaissiere's Greek widow, was winding up his affairs and recouping what he claimed to be owed from the estate. Parkyns' opinion of him is of interest as representing his prejudice against Levantine *évolués* which later became almost obsessional. He never expressed himself more sharply than when describing Ibrahim Kabir. He wrote:

In common decency I would have expected that on the arrival of a European in a place where only three or four were, I should be received willingly into any house for the time being. I, it happened, fell into the shop of a man who always invites European travellers to his hospitality (if they appear rich) and has hence acquired a considerable reputation, and many parting gifts of value from his visitors . . . But when I say travellers, I mean men who came to Egypt with their firman and dragoman, secretary and draughtsman, valet and French cook etc. etc. . . . My friend the Greek had informed him that an Englishman travelling from Abyssinia had arrived at the gin shop, and inquired of him whether he should not invite me to lodge at the house. The master said he would come to see me in the afternoon and in walked a little, thin, pale-faced, effeminate looking young man in Turkish costume with a pipe in his mouth, and, seating himself near me, began by degrees, very politely at first, to make out what I was. I am too old a stalker to be caught in my own business, so I answered in a rather evasive manner, and as politely and meekly as I could.

Parkyns fell short of what the Syrian considered a respectable English traveller should look like, and his assurances that he hoped to obtain some money from Egypt were discounted: the Syrian knew a credit-worthy European when he saw one, and he did not see one in Parkyns. However, he allowed Parkyns to stay in the noisome 'gin shop', where most of the handful of local Europeans came to see him out of curiosity. 'When I returned their calls I was barely requested to be seated, and never offered so much as the usual compliment of a pipe.' Their attitude is more understandable now than it was to Parkyns at the time. The white adventurers and flotsam who made a living for themselves in Khartoum in 1845 had little beyond their Europeanism to give them status. Nevertheless such precarious status as they enjoyed was an achievement of sorts in that it exceeded anything they might have made claim to in their own country. To them, Parkyns was a hopeless failure; incapable even of making the most of his white skin. No one would cash him a bill drawn on his bankers in Alexandria because he carried no letter of credit in French or Italian. Finally he pawned his pistols, that had cost £25 from Westley and Richards, for £3.13s. to a Greek tailor. 'Snip made a great fuss about the matter', he recalled. From the princely sum realized he gave nearly half as a loan to his Greek friend, 'who had been good-natured to me, and was as badly off as myself'. Then he left the 'gin shop' in disgust without being able to make satisfactory alternative arrangements.

> I spent my time in the market-place and coffee-houses, preferring the society of the rude Turkish soldiers to the cold politeness of the Europeans; sleeping with them on the benches of the coffee-houses, dining, like them, on a bit of bread and some cheese or a few radishes, and thus passing my time not at all uncomfortably. I must say that the Europeans I allude to were few in number, and principally the *would-be* great men . . . The fact was, that I, being rather of a careless and easily-satisfied disposition, did not even write to Egypt for a supply till more than three weeks had elapsed. I intended doing so from the first day, but somehow or other each opportunity that occurred of sending a letter slipped past without my catching it – either I was engaged when I remembered it, or out, or lazy, or something of the sort.

Finally, one of his disdainful European acquaintances offered to ensure the delivery of a letter to Egypt, giving Parkyns the impression that he was intent on calling his bluff:

> So I stepped into his house and scrawled a few words on a piece of paper . . . I must own that some of my drafts were rather singular in their appearance. One in particular was handed about for a long while as an object of great curiosity among the London brokers.

However, the one he wrote in Khartoum elicited a prompt response from his banker in Egypt and an Armenian trader in Khartoum was authorized to advance him a considerable sum of money.

> What a change came over my former sneerers! I was an excellent fellow to every one . . . Some of my readers may, perhaps, expect that I refused their invitations; on the contrary, I made the greatest possible friends of all of them, for I felt that, they being civilized men, I had no right to expect any other treatment than I had received, coming among them, as I did, without the necessary passports of a good coat and a full purse . . . I was treated inhospitably by

[125]

no one during all my travels, excepting by Europeans, who had nothing against me but my apparent poverty – a fault which should have made me all the more worthy of their care.

Certainly he was in need of some care, because a mental and physical reaction to his adventures of the previous three years had set in. Letters from England arrived, no doubt urging him to return home, but none has survived. He became absorbed in compiling a record of his stay in Abyssinia, or at least filling in the gaps in his journal caused by the loss of most of what he had written while he was there. With the arrival of his money he was able to ensure a degree of independence by acquiring a mud-brick room of his own.

It was while he was living in this way, that Parkyns was visited by three English undergraduates from Trinity College, Cambridge, who had been his contemporaries during his brief residence there. One of them – Francis Galton, a cousin of Charles Darwin and a polymath of distinction – went to Malta in 1845 to visit a Cambridge friend. He then decided to go to Egypt and on the steamer met two other Trinity men – Montague Boulton, of the Birmingham engineering family, and Hedworth Barclay, of the banking family. Together they did the usual journey up the Nile to Thebes, but while their vessel was tied up near Assuan a boat arrived from the south, and a man disembarked that they took for a Levantine slave dealer. He was Jean d'Arnaud, a French Saint-Simonian socialist who had been employed as an engineer by Muhammed Ali Pasha and had taken part, four years earlier, in one of the attempts to find the source of the White Nile promoted by the Pasha. On Galton's boat, the travellers had a convivial evening together which ended by d'Arnaud persuading the three young men to extend their tour by a five hundred miles' journey across the desert to Khartoum. They set about the task with extraordinary confidence and light-heartedness. It was this journey that began Galton's career as an African traveller that later earned him the gold medal of the Royal Geographical Society.

Having crossed by camel the desert arc of the great loop in the Nile, they arrived at Berber. Galton wrote in his journal:

The local Pasha received us in state and gave us lemonade

from his own limes and it seemed delightful. He also lodged us in a mud house and gave us permission to hire a boat . . . At Khartoum we got (I suppose through the captain of our boat) a mud house facing the blue Nile, across which the dust columns were seen in numbers dancing in the plain. We heard of the existence of a wonderful Frank, probably an Inglese; so we went to see him. We knocked and walked in and there was about the most magnificent physique of a man I have ever seen, half dressed in Arnaout [Albanian] costume, looking quite wild. He turned out to be Mansfield Parkyns recently arrived there after years in Abyssinia. He had been at Trinity College, as well as ourselves, and having taken part in an awkward row, found it best to leave, and had travelled ever since. He put us in the way of all the 'life' in Khartoum and introduced us to the greatest scoundrels I think that could be found anywhere in a room. Men who were too rascally for the Levant or even Cairo. They were slavedealers, outlaws, and I know not what else. Full of stories about how A had been poisoned by B; B having just left the room before the story was told. Parkyns with perfect sang-froid and with all his wits about him, held his own unscathed in this blackguard Bohemia; not a bit sullied by it and much amused.

Having shown his English friends the limited attractions of Khartoum, Parkyns obtained a river-boat and took them for a few days sail up the White Nile where they hoped to get some shooting. Their visit did not interest Parkyns greatly. Galton never forgot it. At the end of his long life, he wrote in his autobiography* his assessment of Parkyns as the traveller 'most gifted with natural advantages for that career' and added, 'He easily held his own under difficulties, won hearts by his sympathy, and could touch any amount of pitch without being himself defiled'.

The unsolved problem of the source of the White Nile was not Parkyns' immediate concern. He was determined to cross Africa, and Khartoum was only a stopping place on his way, where he could equip himself for the next long stage to the west; towards Lake Chad and Bornu. He knew that he would have to

* *Memories of My Life* (Methuen, 1908).

adopt a new style for travelling in the Sudan and places west of it, if he were to ensure uninterrupted progress. His previous successes in his relations with Abyssinians would be of little use to him in dealing with the Muslim authorities along his projected route. On the contrary, any connection with *al-Habash* was best not mentioned; although he still had Gabre Mariam with him. Nor was his liking for peasant dress appropriate; at least, not in the towns. So he bought some smart Turkish clothes and, for urban purposes, assumed that air of sophisticated and somewhat menacing detachment and repose expected of an Ottoman gentleman. Above all, he had money and could cut a dash when necessary, in places where there were no inflationary pressures on prices.

The obstacles before him were likely to be political rather than physical, for although his route across Africa from Khartoum passed over semi-desert country, it was a main route followed for centuries by large numbers of Muslim pilgrims from West Africa on their way to and from Mecca, a journey of several years. For Parkyns, the first stage out of Khartoum would be to El Obeid, the administrative centre for the province of Kordofan, some 300 miles south-west of Khartoum, which had been occupied by Muhammed Ali Pasha's troops for twenty years. To the west of Kordofan was the independent sultanate of Darfur, with its capital at El Fasher, about 350 miles west of El Obeid; a state that had not been visited by Europeans, as far as was known, since W.G. Browne, an Englishman, went there from Egypt across the desert west of the Nile and returned in 1796.

West of Darfur lay the state of Wadai, or Dar Bergu, which had never yet been seen by Europeans. Still further beyond it, were the states of Bagirma and finally of Bornu, to which the British explorers Denham, Clapperton and Oudney had penetrated across the Sahara from Tripoli in 1823. These were remote places viewed from Khartoum in 1846. In distance, the track from El Obeid in Kordofan to Kuka in Bornu was about 1,200 miles. From Parkyns' point of view, the problem was that all these negro Muslim sultanates were suspicious of light-skinned visitors from the Nile as representing possible heralds of the further extension of Muhammed Ali Pasha's empire.

The journey to El Obeid presented him with no problem. If there was one thing the Pasha's functionaries understood, it was their master's insistence that European travellers in his territories should be given protection. Their security was the best possible evidence of the effectiveness of the Pasha's administration compared with that of his Mameluke predecessors, and he never let the European consular representatives in Egypt forget it. He told Richard Milnes when he called on him in December 1843 that, shortly after his appointment as Wali of Egypt in 1805, an English woman had arrived in Cairo wanting to visit the pyramids, a few miles from Cairo across the Nile. To give her the necessary protection from brigands, he had had to send 600 soldiers with her as an escort.

Parkyns had sufficient money to allow him to make a start, but sickness delayed him. All we know of it was a mention in a letter to Richard Milnes two years later: 'I have never', he assured him, 'had an illness except at Khartoum . . . where I was attacked by a sort of cholera which in twenty days carried off several hundreds of the inhabitants'. In *Life in Abyssinia* Parkyns explained his delay in continuing his journey as being due to his 'all but dying from a pestilential fever which kept me for five months on my beam-ends at Khartum'.

He had to find some means of occupying himself until he was fit to travel. Sensibly, he took steps to improve his Arabic and, on the evidence of the improvement of his Arabic calligraphy, he must have worked seriously. This brought him into touch with Sudanese who had received instruction of the traditional Islamic kind, and he admired their style and their learning. In addition, possibly remembering the indigenous manuscripts that Antoine d'Abbadie had collected and shown him at Adwa, he began to collect material for a history of the Sudan, or of Sennar as the region was more usually called at the time. 'I collected', he wrote, 'the fullest particulars of the general history of Nubia, Sennar, and Kordofan. They will work for themselves, if I should ever fancy that the perusal of it would be interesting to the English public'. Apparently he decided that it would not.

Original manuscript historical material is far from plentiful either in Abyssinia or the Sudan, although more has survived there than in West African countries. Parkyns appears to have attempted to overcome this by purchasing, or commissioning, a history from someone who had knowledge of events over the twenty years prior to his visit in Khartoum. It is written in

Italian and entitled 'A History of the Sudan, 1822–1841'. In it appears an account of the Sudanese resistance to the occupation of their country by Muhammed Ali Pasha's army, commanded by his son Ismail. The manuscript remained untouched until 1970 when it was translated and published, with a wealth of valuable commentary by Richard Hill in his book *On the Frontiers of Islam*. It makes a unique contribution to the historiography of the Sudan.

Parkyns' acquisition of the history also indicates the kind of company he was keeping at Khartoum. He kept his aversion for the handful of Europeans, or semi-Europeans, who thought themselves to be persons of importance. He preferred what he called 'the small fry, the assistant surgeons, apothecaries and such like'. One of them, the author of the manuscript history, must also have had sufficient intellect to induce him to undertake the work. On him, Parkyns wrote:

> I met with one friend among them, a poor Levantine-born Neapolitan, who was employed as druggist at the central magazine. While I was at the gin-shop, he was lying dangerously ill in his house. I called on him several times and nursed him a little until he got better. He was very kind to me although he could not assist me much as he received no pay for many months.

Later this same man nursed Parkyns when he was desperately ill; but the Neapolitan author-nurse did not sign his history and his name remains unknown.

The degree of Parkyns' involvement with the European 'small fry' of Khartoum in 1846 is also reflected in an Arabic letter, presumably written by a professional petition-writer, that he received in England seventeen years later from Maria, the Galla widow of a French doctor, Alfred Paney, asking him to intervene in litigation over a house at Khartoum. The letter read:

> We have it firmly in mind that while you were in Khartum, you gave the house to us out of your good nature and generosity . . . and we pray that, out of your goodness and charity, oh my master, you will write to us on the matter . . . and our children in this place send you sincere remembrances and kiss your noble hand . . .

This was by no means the limit to the acquaintances he made, nor their variety. On the one hand, he became friendly with Musa Bey Hamdi, who was acting temporarily in Khartoum for his absent superior Ahmed Pasha Manakli, the governor-general of the Sudan. Parkyns tried, without success, to persuade Musa Bey to take a more lenient view of old Mek Nimr who sought pardon so that he could return from exile on the Abyssinian frontier. However, Musa Bey, formerly one of the white Circassian slaves whom Muhammed Ali Pasha purchased from Turkey to officer his army, was not notable for his mercy. His reputation for ferocity was widespread.

At the other extreme, was an Egyptian who possessed three performing baboons. Parkyns was so interested in the animals that he became the showman's assistant for a time:

> I entered into conversation with him as to their sagacity, the mode of teaching them. and various other topics relating to them. Speaking of his male monkey, he said that he was the most dexterous thief imaginable, and every time he was exhibited he stole dates and other provisions sufficient for his food for the day . . . He begged me to watch for a few minutes . . . near a date-seller, who was sitting on the ground with the basket beside him . . . I could perceive that the monkey had an eye to the fruit, yet so completely did he disguise his intentions that no careless observer would have noticed it . . . In the middle of one of his tricks he suddenly started up from the ground on which he was lying stretched like a corpse, and, uttering a cry as of pain or rage, fixed his eyes full at the face of the date-seller, and then, without moving the rest of his body, stole as many dates as he could hold in one of his hind hands (Apes are not quadru*peds*, but quadra-*mana*.) The date-man being stared out of countenance, knew nothing about the theft till a bystander told him of it, and then he joined heartily in the laugh that was raised against him . . . I have never thought it worth while to teach monkeys of my own any tricks, always preferring to watch their natural actions.

At length, with the rains of 1846 in prospect, Parkyns left for El Obeid in Kordofan. No longer was he the footloose traveller who had arrived penniless in Khartoum in the previous year.

Not only was he better dressed, but he had plenty of money and, while he was in Khartoum, he had been able to correspond with his family and friends in England. Apart from a new rifle and other equipment, Richard Milnes sent him a copy of his poems written during his tour of the Near East – *Palm Leaves* – and also a copy of a recently published English translation of a book on Kordofan by Ignatius Pallme,* a Bohemian by birth, who visited Kordofan on behalf of a merchant house in Cairo in 1838 and 1839. Pallme's book is informative, although tending towards the sensational and not likely to give a modern reader a balanced view of the Turko-Egyptian administration of the period. Parkyns was well able to judge matters of this kind for himself, being also an eye-witness. Reading what Pallme had to say about relations between the Sultan of Darfur and the Turko-Egyptian authorities can have left him in no doubt about the difficulties for him that lay ahead.

To reach El Obeid, he sailed up the White Nile for two days and then travelled by camel. The country of eastern Kordofan is either flat or gently undulating, potentially fertile, thinly provided with umbrella-shaped acacia trees, with glimpses of isolated rocky hills. In the dry season it is shrivelled country but good falls of rain are fairly reliable from June and the villagers can earn a reasonable subsistence from their cultivations, and the collecting of gum arabic from one variety of the acacias. It is not fine country by other than Sudanese standards but more interesting than the plain Parkyns had crossed on his way to Khartoum from Abyssinia.

Muhammed Ali Pasha's expeditionary force from Egypt had occupied Kordofan in 1821, but it was not until twenty years later that he received the Sultan of Turkey's formal recognition of the fact. In 1841 he was addressed as 'Wali of Egypt, including the governments of Darfur, Nubia, Kordofan and Sennar', regardless of the fact that the Sultan of Darfur had never acknowledged his dependence on either Cairo or Istanbul. In effect, the *firman* gave the Pasha the opportunity to intervene in the affairs of Darfur whenever he liked. Sultan Muhammed el Fadl of Darfur was in no doubt that the Egyptians would try to gain control of his territory as soon as the opportunity occurred, and consequently he was suspicious

* *Travels in Kordofan* (London, 1844).

of visitors from Egyptian territory, including Europeans. The Egyptians were equally determined that no firearms should reach the Sultan. One of the Pasha's orders to his officials in Kordofan, with regard to illicit participants in the arms trade, ended: 'If you catch one of them at it, kill him at once'.

The Sultan of Darfur was especially vulnerable to external subversion because he had a large family bred from an unlimited number of wives – over a hundred, it was said. It provided the Egyptians with a wide field for the selection of a pretender, who, with support might become a puppet under their control. This was a tactic that Muhammed Ali Pasha had used twenty years earlier in overthrowing the Sultan of Sennar, then ruler of the Nilotic Sudan. In fact the plan did not develop in respect of Darfur as the Pasha hoped, although awareness of it put the Sultan more than ever on his guard.

While Ignatius Pallme was in Kordofan two of the Sultan's younger brothers escaped there. One was arrested by pursuers and, when taken back to his brother, his eyes were put out. The other – Muhammed Abu Madyan, called 'Abumedina' by Pallme – escaped with a sword wound across his head. On reaching El Obeid, he put himself under the protection of the Egyptian authorities and was given a monthly allowance. Muhammed Ali Pasha, during his visit to the Sudan in 1839, summoned Abu Madyan and promised to place him on the throne of Darfur in return for an annual tribute of a thousand horses, ivory and copper. When he wrote his book Pallme hoped that Abu Madyan would take over in Darfur, because this would open up trade with the country for European merchants; but he added, and Parkyns must have taken note of this:

> At present, any traveller who might reach Darfur would never return, because the reigning sultan looks on every whiteman as a spy of Mehemed Ali's. Mehemed Fadl's chief wish is to have some European settlers in his country; for he is well aware that Mehemed Ali has his eye upon Darfour.

Parkyns knew enough about African tyrants to treat them with caution and he settled down in El Obeid to consider his next move more carefully. The place was then a military centre, with a population estimated at about 12,000. It consisted of six villages or quarters, including one for the official cantonment and barracks, one for the market and one called Kungara where the relics of the previous Darfurian occupation of Kordofan were settled. Parkyns acquired a *tukl* – a circular mud-brick structure with a conical thatched roof – near the market and had it embellished at its apex with empty ostrich eggs for good luck. Stationed there, he could collect intelligence on his future move to the west. Urban amenities in El Obeid were minimal. Of the six mosques in the place, only one was built of brick and none had a minaret; and there was only one coffee shop.

Intelligence on Darfur was not lacking for there was a continual movement of pilgrims and traders through the town and its market. Moreover, Parkyns was soon on good terms with the local Turkish officers and he understood that any plans for Egyptian intervention in Darfur, through the medium of Muhammed Abu Madyan, had been shelved. The activities of the military administration were centred on the collection of taxes and the seizure of slaves from the negro pagans in the Nuba Mountains south of El Obeid. These were needed to meet the needs of Muhammed Ali Pasha's army, partly to provide it with recruits, and partly with a means for paying the troops already serving in lieu of cash. While Parkyns was there, the governor of the province, Mustafa Pasha, received a demand for 5,000 slaves and he mounted the usual raid on the Nuba Mountains to collect them. Parkyns preserved among his papers evidence of this in an Arabic document signed by Yacoub Husni, 'assistant to the Governor' and presumably a Coptic clerk, in which he acknowledged a loan from Parkyns of '2000 Roman piastres' to be repaid 'on our return from the raid'.

It was clear that Parkyns could not make progress by going direct to Darfur and running the risk of being detained there by the Sultan. He decided therefore to see whether he could outflank Darfur from the north by travelling through the southern part of the Libyan desert. And so he left El Obeid as soon as the rains were over and went to live with the Kababish tribe of camel owning nomads living north of El Obeid who were reputed to range far to the west in search of grazing. The Kababish are a group of tribes of Arab origin, with some infusion of Berber blood, that entered the Sudan from the north during the Middle Ages. Among the tribal units can still be recognized historic names from Arabia and North Africa.

Perhaps he could accompany them and find some way of avoiding Darfur, or at least the part of it in which the Sultan's authority was exercised.

The prospect of living in the desert was much more to his liking than sitting in a *tukl* in El Obeid, but he left no proper account of his experiences apart from a lecture he gave to the Royal Geographical Society in 1850. This shows that during the winter of 1846 and the whole of 1847, he was living with the tribe and accumulating a great deal of information about its organization, the customs of its people and the area in which they obtained their subsistence.

There can be no doubt about Parkyns' regard for these nomads, and for their way of life. Yet no one could have had a better opportunity for experiencing their behavioural defects, or the squalor of some aspects of their lives. He acquired his own camels and put his own brand – 'MP' – on their flanks; and good camels they were, too, on the evidence of the picture he painted of himself mounted on one of them. In northern Kordofan, they entered some of the best camel country possible; a vast area of grazing, with adequate supplies of water if properly managed, and free of 'fly'. In addition, there were plenty of slaves to be had as graziers and drawers of water. Intermarriage with indigenous Nubians, and others, darkened their skins and relaxed some of the high-stringing of the true Arab temperament. Politically, their principal requirement was to retain maximum freedom from control by higher sedentary authorities so that they could make the most of their herds in the wide territory that was their range. To outsiders, this gave the impression that they lived in a state of anarchy because their freedom led to intertribal raiding and warfare on a small scale. Over the centuries, the Kababish had prevailed over the Beni Gerar, Dar Hamid and the Zayadia tribes. When Parkyns was with them, skirmishing with the Beni Gerar near the Darfur frontier continued.

Parkyns joined a small tribe which, in those days, was independent of the Kababish leadership. This was a group called Awlad Howal, led by Sheikh Hakim Wad el Dib. Previously they had enjoyed the privilege of providing guides for caravans crossing the desert between El Obeid and Dongola on the Nile, miles to the north. They were also employed as couriers by the Egypto-Turkish authorities on this route.

However, they had fallen foul of a former Turkish governor of Dongola and had moved south towards El Obeid when Parkyns met them. When he moved north himself, he also met the Nurab section that provided then, and still provides, the leadership for the Kababish as a whole and which, in the present century, became rich from the multiplication of its herds and the profitable business of driving herds of camels over the desert to Egypt for sale as meat to the *fellahin*. They were already wealthy, in desert terms, when Parkyns met them and their leader, the famous Sheikh Fadlalla Wad Salim.

He left no precise account of his movements, but, before joining the Awlad Howal, it appears that Parkyns travelled in the vicinity of El Obeid, no doubt with the intention of testing the prospects of his making progress towards Darfur. In the course of doing so he came across encampments of the cattle-owning Arabs of Kordofan; the Baggara. In fact, he had already met Arabs of this kind when he was east of the Nile on his way to Khartoum and, in a moment of nostalgia, he wrote an account in his book of visiting one of their encampments that those who have seen them in more recent times from their motor vehicles will no doubt regard as highly romanticized and idealized.

> We arrived hot and fatigued after a long day's journey, just as the sun was setting. No one but the women and children, and a few infirm old men were in the village, the greater part of the male population being out in the desert with the flocks and herds. As we passed between the rows of huts no one stared at us or made any remarks, but gave a cheerful and kindly answer to our salutation. Neither the mistress of the house we selected, nor an old man who sat at its door, nor any of the neighbours, seemed even surprised at our having come thus uninvited, but welcomed us at once, and, while we were 'kneeling' and unloading our camels, busied themselves, some in preparing refreshments, others in collecting stretchers and mats for our beds; the neighbours volunteering their assistance and the loan of their furniture. As soon as we were seated, two or three patriarchs came to us, and, sitting by us, renewed their expressions of welcome . . . Water sweetened with honey, sour milk, and sundry other cooling beverages were brought in large calabashes by the children of the

house. The old gentlemen took them, and, after tasting them, handed them to us, with 'Ah! this is nice and cool, you must needs be parched; drink, and moisten your lips' . . . I wish I could describe the scene, – the soft doubtful twilight that, for a single instant, separates the glories of a tropical day from the beauties of the night, and which seems to be the signal for all nature to be hushed – not, as with us, gradually and imperceptibly, but at once . . . In the camp innumerable fires were blazing, one or two before each dwelling; over these were grouped the young women of the tribe, busily preparing for the return of their hungry fathers and brethren . . . Should any of my readers wish to paint the scene, they must not forget plenty of strong lights and shades from the fires, and if they can manage to introduce a distant barking of dogs, lowing of cattle, and bleating of sheep, it would greatly add to the truth as well as the interest of the picture . . . Then, after our host had welcomed us, and inquired if his people had treated us properly during his absence, supper for man and beast was supplied in profusion. The people of the house, and many of the neighbours, joining us, and the other families forming in knots near their dwellings, gave our evening meal the appearance of a great picnic party. After a little quiet friendly chat over sundry bowls of new milk the stillness gradually returned to the camp, as its inmates dropped off one by one into the land of dreams. It is a real luxury to be able to sleep out of doors on a warm bright night, with just the least possible breath of air to fan your cheeks. Talk about comfort in a bed-room!

When he decided to explore the possibility of out-flanking Darfur by passing north of it, he rode off towards Dongola, on the loop in the Nile, to join Sheikh Fadlalla Wad Salim of the Kababish. With him went J. Morpurgo, a Jewish Venetian merchant who was visiting Kordofan from Egypt. This was during the rains of 1847, for Parkyns knew that during the rains the Kababish and other camel-owning tribes migrated into the desert away from the Nile according to the pattern of the rainfall. Sometimes the rain would fall in far distant areas to the north of Darfur and create what the Arabs knew as *gizzu*, a generic name for three or four kinds of grass that germinate north and west of Jebel Meidob when rain falls. The Arabs go in search of the *gizzu*, if it exists after the rain water further south has dried up. The animals exist entirely on the goodness and moisture in the grass and are not watered until after they return to the south some months later. Parkyns explained in his lecture:

The rains begin in June and as soon as water is reported to have fallen in the desert, a dromedary rider is sent to explore the truth. If he find no water, or if it be too far, after some days another is despatched, and so on; until one brings notice of water at two or three days distance from the camp. On his return, everyone strikes his tent, collects his baggage on his camels, and old and young, sick and well, prepare for their departure . . . The man who has found the water becomes the guide and goes first with the drums, accompanied by fifteen or twenty young men on dromedaries, and after them follow the women, the laden camels and herds of camels, and then sheep and goats. This order is preserved all day, and in the evening, when the guide announces a halt by beating the drum, everyone alights from his camel and takes the position he occupied during the march. Scarcely have they encamped when the guide remounts and starts off to ascertain more exactly the position since he saw it; for if it be not sufficient for all, the camels can do without water for several days.

In 1847, the *gizzu* had grown and Parkyns went off with the excited young men to ensure that the camels benefited from it. It was a hard life: the cold intense at night, clothing scanty, no fuel or cover and camel's milk the staple support of life. Occasionally, an ostrich egg might be found and fried on a grindstone left in the sun to warm. Sometimes they would hunt down, on the nimbler camels, an ostrich, or one of the fine desert antelopes – white oryx or addax – and by making a circular cut round the hide of their necks they could make the strong ropes for lifting water from the deeper wells.

Parkyns never enjoyed himself more.

I have several times lived on a milk diet for a long period, and once I was 17 days without any sort of nutriment, either bread or meat, except camels' milk, of which I drank several gallons a day. I never was better in my life, and all this time I underwent the most violent exercise . . . How ignorant and stupid are those who exclaim against the hardship of desert life!

However much he enjoyed the experience, it was also made clear to Parkyns that any plan he might have for passing north of Darfur through the southern part of the Sahara was an impractical one and he returned to Dongola; to Mr Morpurgo and the Circassian governor, Musa Bey Hamdi, his former acquaintance at Khartoum.

Shortly after his return to the river, he wrote to Richard Milnes on 20 March 1848 in a manner which showed that he had made up his mind to return to civilization for a spell:

> Pray write me at Alexandria and tell me all the news; or rather leave the news and tell me about yourself. Have your poetic inspirations failed or how is it I hear no more of your works? The former *Palm Leaves* which you sent me are from constant use and fingering become as dark as the natives of this unpoetic soil.

He also went to some lengths to reassure Milnes about his state of mind and his ability to meet hardships he had imposed on himself:

> When you and I were at school, the first few years of birch, rod and caning appeared disagreeable, but at the end of this time all went easily – so it is with me now. The six years are past of schooling and instead of being tired of rambling I am so well accustomed to it now that what formerly was a fatigue is now a pleasure . . . I have just arrived from the desert . . . and I write you all this not as a boast of myself, because, if stupid, at least I have sense enough to know that a good constitution is not a matter of boast, but on the contrary an obligation we owe to the Almighty Creator . . . I need only say (though of course I hope you will keep it secret from my family for the present) that my only intention in returning now to England is to visit my family and friends, to publish if it be considered worth while the sketches I have of my wanderings and to offer my honorary services to my country if they may be considered worthy of acceptance and in as short a time as possible return to any part of Africa which may appear most useful . . . I find that the road to Dar Four is difficult as one is sure to be detained 2 or 3 years if not more

but I have a plan in my head of the success of which I can nearly assure myself . . . I offer two voyages after my return, to follow up the Nile from Egypt to its source or to cross Africa from Dongola to Senegal, through the hitherto unexplored countries North of Darfur. If God grant me the health and strength I have enjoyed since I had the pleasure of seeing you in Egypt, I can succeed in either of these.

The reason for his letter to Milnes was that, on his arrival at Dongola, Musa Bey Hamdi had handed him a letter from Milnes written six months earlier. Such were the postal arrangements in the Sudan. It is apparent that his decision to return to England had set him thinking about how much his years in Africa must have changed him.

I write to you, you see, as an old friend. I hope you consider me as such; if you do not, at any rate you must excuse my familiar style, but I have altogether lost the little good breeding (if notions of Etiquette can be so called) which I may ever have possessed.

Adjustment would be difficult. He had been nineteen when he started his journey and he was now twenty-five. During this period, except for one or two brief interludes, he had seen no fellow-countrymen, nor spoken any English. A few letters had reached him, but only the occasional book and no newspapers. By now, he was speaking colloquial Arabic fluently, probably with a broad Sudan Arab accent. Anyone who spends months in the desert with the voluble young men of the Kababish tribe could hardly do otherwise. Parkyns observed that the townsmen could not stand the Kababish because they talked so loudly. In addition he had become completely accustomed to Arab manners through living all day long under their sway.

It was sensible therefore for him to spend some time in making his way to Cairo, and to spend several months in Egypt before returning to London. Having done his best to patch up a quarrel between Awlad Howal and Musa Bey Hamdi, he set out on his own camels for Egypt, accompanied by Sa'id, whose health was bad, and Gabre Mariam, the Abyssinian servant he had engaged at Adwa. He kept no record of the journey but presumably he covered some of the six hundred miles at Cairo by river. At least he did some paintings of river scenes on the way. When he arrived at the new Shepheard's Hotel in Cairo he cannot have been other than an exotic figure.

There had been some changes in the tourists' part of Cairo round the Ezbekiyah Square since his last visit. It was no longer flooded when the Nile was at its highest and hotel accommodation had developed to meet growing European demand. The firm that had previously managed the overland route through Egypt had been acquired by Muhammed Ali Pasha and was run as a government department by Abdulla Pasha – an English renegade from Northumberland. The big improvement from an English visitor's point of view had occurred shortly before Parkyns arrived. The assistant manager from the primitive place he had stayed in during his previous visit to Cairo – Samuel Shepheard – had opened a new hotel which carried his name, and was situated on the Ezbekiyah Square. Shepheard, who became a friend of Parkyns', had been put ashore from a P & O ship at Alexandria in the year in which Parkyns had originally arrived in Egypt. For a time he worked in a Greek-owned bar until he moved to Cairo. He was a good businessman, as well as a notable character. An American consul described him as 'short, sturdy, strongly-built John Bull of the old type, both in looks and manner, independent and brusque to the very verge of rudeness, and often beyond'. He acquired the site on the Ezbekiyah Square by purchase from Abbas Pasha, Muhammed Ali's grandson, for the price of two whippets called Bess and Ben.

Although the Shepheard's Hotel Parkyns stayed in was a considerable improvement on the previous hotel, it was far from palatial. Shepheard kept a book, known as the Golden Book, that contained, until it was burnt in 1952 with the rest of the old Shepheard's, the observations of those who stayed at the hotel. When Parkyns was there, a discontented English clergyman complained: 'No bed, no bath, no civility'. But it was followed by Parkyns' reply: 'Having remained several months in the hotel, I beg to express the perfect satisfaction I have received in every point of accommodation and civility'. Of course, by his standards, the place must have seemed to provide the ultimate in comfort. To others it did not. Another traveller, a Mr Andrews, for example, thought:

Shepheard's bedrooms are wretched in point of comfort. A

bed so small that it is a danger to sleep in it, a pillow and bolster that would very easily go into a coat pocket; a looking glass that shows one eye up at the top of the glass and the other eye at the bottom; windows that won't shut when open, and won't open when shut.

However, these were months that gave Parkyns some opportunity for finding his feet again. Staying at the hotel were a number of men that Parkyns found congenial. For example, the German Baron J.W. von Müller, who had recently completed some considerable journeys in Morocco and Algeria during which he had been made a prisoner by the Amir Abdel Kadar. 'Though but a harmless naturalist,' he said, 'I was treated as a French spy, and was near losing my head, which was the fate of my companion.' Parkyns discussed his future plans with him. Then there was a colonel from the Indian army who was recuperating from sickness – James Outram, the Bayard of India, who was a man to appreciate Parkyns.

However, the man who became a lifelong friend was a Royal Navy captain, Henry Murray, whose older brother, Charles Murray, was the British Consul-General in Egypt. They were the sons of the Earl of Dunmore; clubable men of no great distinction in their professions. Indeed, Charles Murray who, in his early days, had been a Fellow of All Souls, earned the description from Disraeli of 'the stupidest diplomat I have known', when, after being transferred from Cairo to Tehran, he brought about the Persian War almost single-handed. Outram commanded the expedition from India that was sent to deal with the situation. Henry Murray was not exposed to temptations in the public service that might lead to error. He had seen little service afloat and had become a popular figure in London society. He and Parkyns went up the Nile to visit the antiquities and also to Suez and Sinai, using Parkyns' own camels.

Parkyns' second visit to Suez was made in the course of his search for the bird skins he had collected in Abyssinia and endeavoured to send back to England. The largest consignment of twelve hundred birds had been sent from Massawa to Aden on the German brig commanded by Captain Rödatz who had met Parkyns at Adwa. From Aden they had been shipped, four years earlier, to Hamburg and had not been heard of since. They were in fact in a warehouse at London docks. When they were ultimately retrieved he found that two hundred of the brightest coloured birds had been pilfered. A second consignment of bird and animal specimens, arms, costumes and the like, had been sent unaccompanied to Aden and remained there for four years. When they were finally located, one case was sent to Parkyns in Cairo but the contents had been destroyed by rats. The second case disappeared altogether:

> Thus I lost a most valuable collection, for it consisted principally of birds which I do not now possess, and of some very rare and beautiful monkeys, besides the other curiosities. A third collection, from Nubia and the White Nile, which I had left in Egypt, arrived safe and in good condition . . . It consisted of about six hundred birds, and about a ton weight of nigger arms and implements.

His friendship with the Murray brothers was useful to Parkyns at this juncture because it gave him a link with official circles in Cairo and London and, through Henry Murray, with the Royal Geographical Society of which he was an active member. So when Parkyns arrived in London in the summer of 1849, there was nothing to delay his making plans for the future African journeys he had in mind. Richard Milnes was still a bachelor and living at his chambers at 160 Pall Mall. Henry Murray was at 9 Albany. Naturally Parkyns was something of a celebrity in the tightly-knit society of the London clubs, and was looked to as an authority on what had become one of the leading geographical problems of the day, the sources of the White Nile.

10

Beset by the wrangling between Charles Beke, d'Abbadie, Ayrton, Cooley, McQueen and others, about the sources of the White Nile, Dr Norton Shaw, at the RGS, must have looked forward to meeting Mansfield Parkyns. His reputation had preceded him, and if anyone seemed likely to make a serious attempt to solve the problem, it was he.

Parkyns too had his problems with rival explorers, although not of his making. There was nothing more disagreeable to him than contention and duplicity, and in the letter he wrote to Dr Shaw on 30 September 1849, there was a suggestion that he was being exposed to both:

> A letter I received yesterday from Egypt informed me of an expedition preparing for the discovery of the sources of the White Nile, under the auspices of Mons. D'Abbadie the elder, and Baron Müller, a German. This idea entered the head of the latter gentleman, from his having heard of my intending the same plan on my return from England, whither I thought it necessary to repair for a short time to recruit my health and arrange a few notes I had collected during my 8 years absence ... Now I don't think it right that these

gentlemen should cut me out and enter the field before me as the idea was originally my own. Therefore I take the liberty of writing to you to offer myself for these countries as quickly as possible . . . As for the necessary funds etc., knowing as I do that govt is never ready to advance any discovery, however interesting, where it may cost the country a farthing, I am prepared to incur every expense myself rather than forego the chance of being as far as my humble powers allow my being useful to my country and science. Should the plan I have formed of taking boats up the course of the Nile not meet with your entire approbation I should be happy to undertake any other expedition you might propose in Africa.

He was invited to discuss the matter with the president of the society – Captain W.H. Smyth, RN – and Dr Norton Shaw made the helpful suggestion that he might consider the unemployed Dr Bialloblotsky, then in Cairo, as a potential travelling companion. Shortly afterwards, news arrived that Baron von Müller, unaccompanied by Antoine d'Abbadie, had already left Cairo for the Sudan to ascend the river south of Khartoum. This he had failed to do, and Parkyns decided to return to his earlier plan of crossing Africa to the Atlantic. There was less urgency for him to make a start.

In the meantime, he took delivery of what remained of his collection of bird skins and, instead of returning to Africa, he spent much of the winter of 1849 preparing them for finishing by a professional taxidermist. When in London, Richard Milnes included him in his social life, during which he met the publisher John Murray and discussed with him the form a book on his travels should take. He would write first about Abyssinia and separately about the Sudan and Egypt. By the end of 1849, three hundred pages were in the publisher's hands.

None of these tasks had been completed when he left once more for the east in the summer of 1850; not for Cairo, but for Constantinople. Either to give him a career, or to provide him with a status that might help him during his forthcoming travels, a position in the diplomatic service had been obtained for him.

Since joining the Liberals, Richard Milnes had improved his relations with Lord Palmerston who, in 1850, was Foreign Secretary to Lord John Russell's administration. There is no direct evidence of Milnes' intervention on Parkyns' behalf, but he certainly introduced him to Palmerston and, not long afterwards, Parkyns was posted as an assistant secretary at the embassy at Constantinople. The appointment carried with it inclusion in the diplomatic service, a body that numbered no more than 125 members at the time. His name continued to appear in the Foreign Office List for the rest of his life, although he was not actively employed for over forty years. The appointment is not without its mystery.

An assistant secretary at Constantinople in 1850 was known as a *dragoman*, or interpreter. Traditionally, the *dragomans* were recruited from Greek families, resident in the capital on the Bosporus, that spoke the necessary languages and were versed in the extraordinary protocol and practices of such key Ottoman institutions as the Grand Seraglio and the Sublime Porte. These Levantine specialists were also suspected of being experts in matters of corruption and deception, hotly though they denied it.

Some ambassadors trusted them: Stratford Canning, the ambassador in 1850 – the Great Elchi – did not, and he asked the Foreign Office to try recruiting young Englishmen to replace the traditional *dragomans* – Englishmen of good birth and education, preferably from Thomas Arnold's Rugby, who would learn Turkish, Arabic and Persian, but not corruption and deceit. Their rank was that of 'assistant secretary'. However, the scheme, which included Parkyns' appointment, did not succeed, and well before his retirement, Canning had turned once more to the Levantine *dragomans* he had previously distrusted.

Parkyns, being already familiar with some of the required languages, and having demonstrated his gifts for getting on with all kinds of people, and for keeping his head in unusual circumstances, must have seemed a promising candidate. Apart from his languages and personal qualities, he had seen the southern parts of the Ottoman realm – the Red Sea area, including Massawa – which were remote from Constantinople. When Etienne Pisani, one of a dynasty of indigenous *dragomans* at the British embassy, was asked about the status of Massawa, he had to confess that he did not know; and it was rare indeed for a Pisani to plead ignorance.

On the other hand, the suitability of Parkyns' temperament

for the life of a diplomat or bureaucrat was questionable, and it is hard to believe that this was not evident to those concerned with his appointment. Perhaps it was intended that his official post should be nominal and used to facilitate his plans for exploration. Considerations of this kind were not unknown to Palmerston in special circumstances; but there is no direct evidence that this is what he intended for Parkyns.

Trouble was inevitable, for Sir Stratford Canning could not be expected to approve of Mansfield Parkyns, nor he of Canning. The ambassador was a tall, exceptionally good-looking man who adopted a lofty manner. This is not to imply that he used his appearance entirely as a substitute for professional competence and basic intelligence. According to his biographer:

> Canning the man, with his perfect grace, his manners of the old school curtesy, his tone of *preux chevalier*, possessed a charm which was felt by all who were capable of appreciating so refined and exalted a nature. The image of the Queen of England, the embodiment of the country he loved, he was a majestic personage and he certainly earned the reputation of arrogance and even of vanity by such pretensions ... The Turks might respect his honest truthfulness, but when it took the form of plain-spoken reprimand, they began to wish for a little polite insincerity.

As Kinglake put it: 'They felt that he humbled them by making his dictation clearly apparent'.

Nor did Canning make friends among his own staff: 'it is said that one of them never held converse with his Excellency without keeping a grasp on the door-handle, ready for instant escape'. He overworked them and expected them to do the dullest of clerical work with enthusiasm. Although devoted to the reform of Ottoman institutions, Canning never liked Constantinople, and he told one newly-arrived member of his staff: 'Be friendly with the great men, but never intimate with them. Somehow intimacy with a Turk is almost an impossibility'. Intimacy with the lower classes, which Parkyns enjoyed, was even less desirable.

Clearly, this was the opposite of Parkyns' style and partiality, and one wishes one could record that he had an interview with the Great Elchi before he left, in which he expressed his opinion of this ambassadorial monstrosity with the frankness of which he was capable. At all events, he was back in London in the following year. It is likely that he suffered ill-health at Constantinople, although this might have been his only act of diplomacy there. All that has survived to recall his brief employment as a diplomat appeared in *Life in Abyssinia*, in which he took the opportunity of contrasting the Turks he liked as representatives of their own culture with those that had adopted European *mores* and were Canning's candidates for leadership of reformed Turkey.

Parkyns wrote:

I have lived much among Turks of every nation and class – more, I am happy to say, among the uncivilized than the civilized; and here is the comparative description I should give of them: – *Uncivilized Turk*: middle-sized; of powerful frame; blunt but sincere in character; brave; religious, sometimes even to fanaticism; cleanly, temperate, addicted to coffee and pipes; fond of a good blade, and generally well skilled in its use; too proud to be mean, cowardly, or false; generous to prodigality; and in dress fond of bright colours and rich clothing, of which he often wears three of four suits at a time, one over the other. – *Civilized Turk*: under-size; of delicate frame; polite, but insincere; not over-brave; often boasting of atheism; neglecting the ablutions of his religion, partly because the Franks are dirty, and partly because his new costume won't admit of them; given to Cognac and cigarettes; fond of a showy sheath if a 'militaire', or of a pretty cane if a civilian; no pride whatever, but lots of vanity; possesses no Oriental generosity; and for dress wears a frock coat, stays to give a small waist, a gay-coloured 'gent's vest', ditto ditto inexpressibles, often of a rather '*loud* railway pattern', and strapped down very tight; his head-dress is a ridiculously small red scullcap, worn at the back of the head, and often containing a small piece of looking-glass, whereby on all occasions to arrange the rather unruly coarse hair it frequently covers. Straw-colour Naples imitation gloves and an eyeglass, are generally considered as indispensable parts of the 'getting up alla Franca'. In point of manners, the lowest *real* Turk is a nobleman; the best of the Europeanized lot is barely a gentleman.

His dislike for 'westernized' Turks is understandable for he came from a class of Englishman who believed that everyone 'should do his duty in that state to which it had pleased God to call him'. If Parkyns was aware of this in dealing with his London tailor, how much further did he go astray in comparing a westernized Turk with Turks who had neither the temptation nor the opportunity for compromising their inherited traditions. What Parkyns really resented was that a minor Turkish functionary who achieved literacy in a European language – no mean feat – should then feel entitled to assume a place and bearing in his adopted Western society higher than that to which a minor Western functionary of similar status would aspire.

Back at Ruddington, at his brother's house, Parkyns pressed on with his book. The Parkyns family was experiencing financial problems following the death of Lord Rancliffe, the head of the family, who left the whole of his estate to his mistress. Mansfield became restless for he was considering a proposal for joining an expedition to the American Rockies, and he maintained his taste for the rough life, if local tradition is to be believed, by sleeping on the floor of his bedroom with a block of wood for a pillow and with Gabre Mariam sleeping across the threshold.

However, Parkyns decided to finish the book before undertaking anything else, and he worked hard until he was thoroughly tired of it. John Murray was helpful and, in writing parts of it, Parkyns may have had the assistance of Francis Galton. What interested him in it, as its author, and what the publisher judged would make the book saleable, led to debate. Murray wanted him to include more anecdotes of his African experiences: Parkyns was more interested in his recollections of the peoples he had met and their customs. He told John Murray:

I send a few sheets on the domestic manners and customs, being the part in which were observed some sentences considered to be 'not quite sufficiently delicate' . . . On the other hand, as regards your cutting out some pieces, I quite agree with you in taste, although I fear I shall get myself blamed by some of my female friends.

[149]

Life in Abyssinia appeared in November 1853 in two handsome volumes. It was dedicated to Lord Palmerston and illustrated by engravings of Parkyns' own drawings and watercolours. It contained a useful map compiled by Arrowsmith. Milnes said he would review it for the *Edinburgh Review*, but nothing appeared. Nor did the *Quarterly Review* notice it, although published by John Murray. Most critics thought Parkyns lacking in earnestness and his book flippant about serious matters. For example, his chapter on missionaries; his comments on British and European *mores* abroad; his satisfaction with aspects of primitive life that were better not mentioned. The critics' attitude in general was that he had 'let the side down'. We do not know what Lady Palmerston said to Parkyns about it, but her comment to Richard Milnes reflected what respectable people thought. 'Venables', she wrote, 'approves Parkyns' book, calling it the most successful attempt by a man to reduce himself to the savage state on record'.

The most pungent review appeared in *Blackwood's* from the pen of Frederick Hardman, a foreign correspondent of *The Times* with intellectual pretensions, who claimed to be an expert on Africa, of which he knew nothing at first hand, through reviewing books on African exploration. For him, Parkyns was a heaven-sent chopping block. Hardman began:

> Locomotion, profitless and often aimless is a condition of an Englishman's existence ... Mr. Mansfield Parkyns is an amateur barbarian ... Fancy a civilised Englishman, gently nurtured and educated, pitching his tent for three years amongst filfthy savages, adopting their dress and usages ... having himself partially tattooed, eating raw beef ... gashing his flesh in order to produce scars and protuberances ... and upon his return home, coolly publishing his confessions ... as if he would say, See what a fine fellow I am to have thus converted myself into a greasy, shoeless savage ... We are much mistaken, or Mr. Parkyns will be the cynosure of all eyes during the approaching spring – particularly if he condescends occasionally to exhibit his tattooed arm, and to bolt a raw beef-steak.

Most wounding of all was Hardman's comment on a passage in which Parkyns had boasted of being 'the d'Orsay of Adowa'. So he had; with his tongue in his cheek. In describing how he lived the part of an Abyssinian gentleman about town, Parkyns had written:

It was the only period in my life in which I ever felt myself a really great man. I 'cry very small' in England, with a much greater expenditure. The men will not look after me with admiration, nor the girls make songs about me here.

It was a perfectly factual statement on which Hardman commented: 'Innumerable incidents in your Abyssinian career deserve to be commemorated in flowing metre, and sung by Ethiopian serenaders to banjo accompaniment, and to the ancient and pathetic melody of "The King of the Cannibal Islands".'

Others tried to be kinder. One referred to his 'humorous, rollicking, letter-writing style'. Another assured him that his style was 'spirited, racy, and abundantly good for the subject', and that his narrative was 'highly interesting'. Another remarked: 'What an amusing book this is, and what an agreeable savage is Mansfield Parkyns'. None of them showed the least interest in a book about Abyssinia which broke new ground, and which, in many chapters, was well informed and well written.

Parkyns was hurt. He had been quite sincere in his reactions to contact with Abyssinians and Sudanese, and disarmingly frank in describing them to the public. But the Mid-Victorian middle classes were unappreciative of this kind of thing. Nevertheless, the book was quite a success both in England and America where it was reviewed in over twenty magazines and papers. One imagines that many outside the literary clique took a more tolerant view of Parkyns' ingenuousness. He wrote in his introduction:

I do not fear criticism. On the contrary, I put myself in the most humble attitude before the mighty wielders of the pen, and plead – that to attack my style would be unmanly, and betray want of good manners on their part; for it would be as bad to quiz a foreigner because he could not speak good English; I don't profess to be a writer any more than he would pretend to be a Briton.

He ended his introduction with an apt quotation from Pickwick:

Numerous scenes, of which I had no previous conception, have dawned upon me, I hope to the enlargement of my mind and the improvement of my understanding. If I have done but little good, I hope I have done less harm, and that none of my adventures will be other than a source of amusing and pleasant recollections to me in the decline of life. God bless you all!

In the meantime, he found time to acquire a residence of his own in the shape of Woodborough Hall in a valley village between Nottingham and the cathedral town of Southwell, where he understood that coal might be found. There, he became the enthusiastic farmer of 450 acres and a horticultur-alist of some reputation since he was invited to judge for the Royal Horticultural Society. As he observed in a letter to Monckton Milnes: 'I am one of those people who strives to do well what I take in hand'. His difficulty was that he could not organize his time sufficiently. During his rare visits to London, what he enjoyed most was to call on Dr Norton Shaw and gossip with him in the rooms of the RGS, now transferred to a house in Whitehall Place; but his correspondence with Mr Shaw is punctuated with apologies for not keeping appoint-ments and for failing to call on him. However, there was some excuse for his negligence, for he confessed, in a letter to Dr Shaw in 1852:

> The fact is that I have been and still am in search of that almost indispensable organ, my heart . . . I shall tell you who the person in question is, I *hope* shortly, but I cannot tell, for nothing whatever is settled in any way.

Any prospects of his returning to Africa either to cross the continent, or to discover the source of the Nile, was receding.

The young lady who had made away with Mansfield's heart at such an inconvenient moment was Emma Louisa, third daugh-ter of Sir Richard Bethell QC, one of the most highly-rewarded advocates of the day. Already he was Solicitor-General and he was later to become Lord Chancellor with the title of Lord Westbury.

Richard Bethell's daughters were celebrated for their good looks, the best remembered being Emma Louisa's elder sister

Augusta. She was the beauty who haunted Edward Lear to such an extent that he never mustered the courage to propose to her. Eventually, she married a complete cripple and Lear remained a bachelor; yet further evidence, people said, of the eccentricity inherent in the Bethell family. Richard Bethell himself was more accomplished than eccentric, and was regarded as a most daring advocate, with a turn of phrase which was both pungent and original. The most widely quoted of the many courtroom stories about him concerned a trial before an ecclesiastical court during which he described the judgment of the bishops as 'oily and saponacious and therefore difficult to grasp'; a quip that caused Bishop Wilberforce of Oxford to acquire the nickname of 'Soapy Sam'. On another occasion, he told a judge, if he had understood him rightly, 'that his lordship would be turning the matter over in what he is pleased to call his mind'.

Mansfield was head-over-heels in love with Louisa, and presumably she with him, because her parents can hardly have regarded him as other than a suitor of questionable suitability. However, it is evident, from later correspondence, that Richard Bethell developed a good opinion of Parkyns. In any case, his consent to his daughter's marriage was not long delayed, although he is said to have required an assurance from Parkyns that he would not again go exploring in Africa. The ceremony took place in January 1854 at the tiny church at Winslade, across the Winchester road outside Hackwood Park. A fashionable London wedding was the last thing Parkyns wanted.

Thereafter, nothing could tempt him from Woodborough to London, although he had been elected to the council of the RGS, nor to accept more than a few of Richard Milnes' invitations to his celebrated house-parties at Fryston Hall near Pontefract at one of which Parkyns met Richard Burton.

He worked hard at his farming and the improvement of his house. However, he was not left in the enjoyment of his new-found domesticity for long.

In the year of his marriage, the first rumblings of the Crimean War began when some Roman Catholic monks attempted to place a silver star over the manger in the church of Christ's Nativity in Bethlehem. They were opposed by monks of the Orthodox Church, a number of whom were killed. Tsar Nicholas II claiming himself to be the protector of the

Orthodox Church invaded from his base at Sebastopol. By the following spring, Britain had allied with Napoleon III to thwart him and a British Expeditionary Force embarked for the Crimea. Mansfield Parkyns had already joined the local Volunteers, which was now mustered for home defence, having been recommended to do so years before by Richard Milnes when they were sailing together up the Nile in Egypt.

Parkyns took his soldiering seriously. Writing to John Murray 'in a muddle', he explained:

> owing to the machinations of that Muskovite Prince of abomination and others, I am ordered with the Notts Militia on permanent duty . . . This state of things is by no means pleasant, just when a man is, after a wandering life, beginning to enter fully into the happiness of domestic quiet, but it would never do to shirk at such a critical moment . . . I have no subaltern to assist me in the internal economy of 86 'roughs' and we have 8 hours drill per diem . . . I have almost succeeded in persuading the men that it is not quite soldier-like to fight and swear loudly at one another in the ranks!

Like most activities he undertook, Parkyns did his work with the militia well and, five years later, when the force was reorganized, he was promoted from Captain to Lieut. Colonel and given command of the 8th Sherwood Foresters, the original militia battalion of the famous regiment.

In 1855 there occurred a death in the family which would be remembered with lifelong regret. Louisa gave birth to a son who died in infancy. Thereafter she had eight daughters in succession. Mansfield Parkyns was enveloped in family life, while Livingstone, Burton, Speke and Baker were all at work in East Africa and on the Nile. A new phase in African exploration had begun and European relations with the continent were changing.

Although Parkyns' residual interest in Africa was mainly nostalgic, he remembered the continued presence there of his old travelling companions John Bell and Walter Plowden. In *Life in Abyssinia* he assured his readers that

> I cannot help saying how sorry I was to part from them, – how much I look forward to seeing them even now . . . and do what we have often done before, – eat a raw beefsteak, and enjoy it for the sake of the good company.

In fact he learned nothing of them until his return to London in 1849. There is no evidence that he was in correspondence with them even then, but from time to time news must have reached him, through Dr Shaw of the Royal Geographical Society, of their fortunes in the intervening years.

Walter Plowden had returned to England and obtained the post of consul at Massawa; he was encouraged to limit his activities to the expansion of trade between Britain and the Abyssinian highlands. He set off at the end of 1847 to take up his post with a salary of £500 per annum, £200 for house rent and £200 for an interpreter. Bell returned to Debra Tabor to live under the patronage of Ras Ali of Begemder.

By 1854, the year of Parkyns' marriage, the name of Kassa was cropping up more and more in the affairs of Amhara. Kassa was a successful aspirant to power, who was related to men of consequence in their day. He had been partly educated in a monastery, acquiring literacy in Ethiopic and familiarity with the traditions of Abyssinian history, and he had had the valuable experience of being in action against Egyptian forces trained on European lines. Later, he had become *shifta*, that is to say he had stepped outside the law and formed his own force of rebels. Since he was a man of quick wit, ambition, energy and ruthlessness, he dominated the existing chieftains and, in a remarkably short time, emerged as the Emperor Theodore.

It was a complicated story and one which Plowden reported to the foreign office as it unfolded. He wrote well, for he was in a position to observe events at first hand. He described Theodore as resembling other highland Abyssinians, his skin almost black and his features more Caucasian than Negroid. He wore his hair plaited close to his head and going back from his high forehead. In build, he was light but wiry; quick in movements; given to travelling on foot with his men, and jumping into his saddle when mounting. His dress was simple except when he was panoplied for battle or participating in ceremonies. His 'palace' was usually of wood and grass, except when he settled in Gondar before he had the place destroyed. All agreed that his good manners were notable; 'He salutes the meanest subject with courtesy,' Plowden wrote, 'and he is generous to excess.'

However, in a rage, often for unpredictable reasons, the king was terrifying. In the next twelve years of his life, there would

[155]

be many to confirm this among the survivors of his negligent attitude to the sanctity of human life.

It would be too much to suppose that Plowden or any other European really understood what was going on, or understood the Emperor Theodore. Certainly the overworked clerks in the Foreign Office were disinclined to take much interest in the subject. They were fully occupied by the Crimean War; the climax, to date, of the Eastern Question.

Theodore's victory over Ras Ali in 1856 meant much realignment of allegiances among the Europeans. Bell had to take sanctuary in a church because he had been with Ras Ali when he suffered defeat at the hands of Theodore's men.

Plowden was about to go on leave to England when news of Theodore's final victory reached Massawa. He changed his plans and went inland as fast as he could to pay his respects to the new emperor. Bell also was released from sanctuary to join the new monarch's retinue. Both Englishmen were impressed by the vigorous and visionary self-made man who seemed to be the solution to long years of insecurity. At last the Christian population had a leader who could master the pseudo-Muslim Galla war-lords. Theodore began his reign with all the revolutionary vigour to be expected of him, and it would be wrong to suppose that there was cynicism in what he did simply because there was no possibility of his reforms being carried out. In intention, he abolished slavery; he laid down an official dogma for a church that thrived on dissension; he questioned the prerogatives of consuls. He desired to send embassies abroad to treat with 'great European Powers on equal terms'. He put Bell to drilling Abyssinian musketeers on European lines; and he even tried to build, on Lake Tana, an imitation steamer of papyrus grass 'with a couple of wheels affixed to the sides of each, to be turned by a handle like that attached to a common grindstone'. About a hundred men embarked to work it. Not surprisingly, it sank.

In these circumstances it was difficult for Europeans to do other than doubt the Emperor Theodore's sanity; but there was no doubting the qualities that brought him success. His main achievement, in terms of the progress of his country, was the overthrow of the Muslim Galla war-lords who had divided the Christian areas of population between them. This he achieved by military means, but many of the Christian leaders were not prepared to suffer a military dictatorship, any more than they had in past centuries. Theodore's reforms in the field of government were quite ineffective. Nevertheless, the fact that he had such ideas mark him off from the general run of Abyssinian rulers. Where did he get these ideas? Where did he acquire his alleged acquaintance with Shakespeare, and his knowledge of world affairs?

Most of our information comes from indigenous chroniclers, consular correspondence, missionaries, and journalist travellers. Nearly all of it is of questionable historical reliability, even when it records direct observation. European observers give the credit for broadening Theodore's awareness of the outside world to John Bell and, particularly, to Walter Plowden. Plowden was suspect in Theodore's eyes because he mistrusted consular privileges. Bell, however, became a close companion for he had completely identified himself with Abyssinian life; he had accepted the Coptic faith, and received the office of *lekwamakwas*, or chamberlain, to the Emperor.

All this is the province of historians who will continue to sift and argue the evidence for years to come. What did Parkyns make of it?

He had not heard of Theodore while he was in Abyssinia, or at least he made no mention of him. This is not suprising, because while he was in the country Theodore was still making his way as a brigand among the valleys west of Lake Tana that lead to the plains of the Sudan. When he heard about Theodore's rise to power, he saw it as a familiar process. Without reading the local chronicles, he was well aware of the process by which changes in government were brought about. It was not peculiar to Abyssinia by any means, but the mountainous topography of the country made rebellion against established authority much less dangerous there than elsewhere. A daring man, either from plain ambition of the righting of some real or supposed wrong, had only, in Parkyns' words, 'to buy a drum and hire a few followers to start a rebellion'. If he had success in highway robbery, his following increased and the objects of attack would become more important. If success mounted further, the rebel would become more respectable in his claims, until he became a serious contender for the rule of his territory. Parkyns felt that Theodore was no more than a supreme example of this process and recognized that he might be a man of character without being a man likely to introduce enlightened government into Abyssinia.

He was not far wrong. Theodore soon faced rebellions against his own rule, and he reacted with traditional ferocity and personal predilection.

Walter Plowden continued to report these developments, as he saw them, to the Foreign Office, in despatches that have become an important source of information for the period. However, when the Liberals were in office in 1860, Lord John Russell became suspicious of events and peremptorily ordered Plowden to return to Massawa and stop dabbling in Abyssinia's domestic affairs. It was while he was complying with this order that Plowden was attacked by *shifta* close to Gondar and mortally wounded. During the ensuing campaign of revenge, Bell also lost his life.

Shortly before Bell left on the expedition against Plowden's killer, in which he himself was killed, one of the Protestant missionaries met him and left one of the few surviving accounts of how he lived at Theodore's camp:

> We came to a sooty but nocturnal abode of the Anglo-Abyssinian noble. A doorway of a few slender canes brought us into a most dirty, foul and smoky lair.

Bell invited him in:

> 'Here is a hand, and if you object to the obnoxious fumes, a well-fitted pipe is a sure antidote,' he explained in a laughing cheerful voice.

When Mr Stern asked why he did not live out in the open, Bell replied:

> 'Pooh, pooh! don't lecture me on the luxuries of dews and blue skies, to which I am condemned eight months out of my twelve; but squat down here on a skin free from all the living attractions while I pour you out, in this half-broken cup, the only china in my possession, something which, I have not forgotten the good old tongue, "cheers but not inebriates".' I obeyed and passed away about an hour in listening to my friend's ludicrous comparison of the happy existence in savagedom, with the exquisite miseries inflicted by the absurd conventionalities of civilisation.

[158]

Shortly afterwards, Stern met Bell at a church service, after which Bell asked the German missionary Flad

> to become the guardian and executor of his will should the next battle-field terminate his career . . . three months later, this brave and kind-hearted man, to the regret of the whole nation, nobly fell in defending the life of his Sovereign and friend.

Making allowances for sentimentality and the editorial licence of those bringing Stern's account to press, Bell certainly left behind a good reputation, and a family whose descendants are still identifiable. Stern's account must have seemed more recognizable to Parkyns when he read it than all the nonsense that appeared in papers and books by people who had never seen Abyssinia.

There were others in Abyssinia to whom Parkyns' thoughts must have turned during these troubled times. His only son by his Abyssinian marriage was born shortly before he left for the Sudan. According to family tradition transmitted through Parkyns' great grandson, Ato Ambaye Gezeheyn, Parkyns left behind a document directing that his son should be allowed to visit England on reaching the age of eighteen. The boy was brought up with his mother's family at Addaro. When he grew up, some of the ex-soldiers who had followed his father joined him. He took possession of the two rifles Parkyns had left behind him. Their names were Waterloo and Grass. Ambaye says that when he was young he saw one of these rifles in his grandfather's rifle rack. It was a short rifle with a brass barrel and a decorated wooden stock. Some letters, including the precious letter directing Parkyns' son to England, were destroyed in a village fire. Consequently when the time came for him to set out on his journey, he had no written evidence of his parentage.

In the mean time, the Emperor Theodore had seized power in the country, determined to bring about the unity it had lacked for so many years. Bell and Plowden had been killed, and the restraint they are credited with exercising over Theodore's visionary schemes had been removed. Even before their deaths the Emperor had found his martial talents insufficient for his purpose. Bedevilled by internal revolt and apprehension of Muslim aggression, he sought European help in the simple belief that his Christian co-religionists would respond to his appeals. With this in mind he wrote to Queen Victoria without being aware that the government in London had already decided that they had no interest in Abyssinia and certainly no desire to become involved in its problems. It was, to say the least, an unfortunate interpretation of this policy to omit sending a reply to the Emperor's letter. Theodore was deeply embittered by this slight. He arrested Plowden's successor as British Consul and other Europeans in the country. Subsequently the members of a mission sent by the British government to obtain their release were also arrested and all the prisoners incarcerated in the mountain fortress of Magdala.

It was at this juncture that John Parkyns, known locally as Bashai Johannes – decided to leave his war-torn country to join his father in Nottinghamshire. He was intercepted by the Emperor's men and, being regarded as a European, he too was despatched over the mountains to be detained at Magdala. It was probably there that he learnt his English from the captive missionaries. It was there also that he met the daughter of the German botanist Schimper, whom he later married.

In 1868 the prisoners at Magdala were released by General Napier's relief expedition in a campaign that cost £9m. and involved British troops in a march of some 800 miles over stony mountain tracks. Fortunately they were not involved in much fighting. Their route lay through the territory of Ras Kassai of Agame – the second cousin of Mansfield Parkyns' wife Tures – who remained neutral. Later he became the Emperor John IV, a man of great importance to the modern history of his country.

John Parkyns married and returned to his village. Later, when the Italians invaded Abyssinia and suffered their appalling defeat at Adwa in 1896, John Parkyns acted as intermediary between the Italian and Abyssinian commands. As a result he went to live behind the Italian frontier in Eritrea, where he died in about 1916, a respected and well-disposed man.

Mansfield Parkyns, of course, knew nothing of this. When Napier's Abyssinian campaign began in 1868, he wrote some letters to the papers and gave a lecture on the country to the Royal United Services Institute. Needless to say, its style was in marked contrast to the usual sober dissertations members were accustomed to hearing. He had declined to join the expedition on the grounds that many Abyssinians were his friends and that he had no intention of fighting them. There is no record of what he may have felt when the first official list of the prisoners freed at Magdala was released and included the name of John Parkyns. Friends intervened to save him embarrassment and the name was deleted from subsequent lists.

Parkyns had now become a Victorian paterfamilias. He and his wife had settled at Woodborough Hall and lived quietly while their family grew remorselessly. At first they were comfortably off because Emma had received a substantial marriage settlement from her father. (He gave her younger sister £20,000). There is little to show how they lived except for one or two recorded events. For example, Parkyns took command of the Thorneywood Chase company when the volunteers were reactivated in 1859 in response to Napoleon III's sabre-rattling. When the volunteer movement was reorganized soon afterwards, he became the first commander of the 8th Battalion, Sherwood Foresters. He also gave more time to his talents as a wood carver and one wonders whether the splendid Victorian carvings at Hackwood Park, his father-in-law's residence near Basingstoke, were an inspiration for the impressive work he did at Woodborough. He maintained a well-equipped workshop in which the villagers interested in carving could work.

Richard Bethell, Mansfield's father-in-law, became Lord Chancellor in 1861, taking the title of Lord Westbury and, with the patronage he commanded, he arranged for Mansfield Parkyns to obtain a post in the Bankruptcy Court. By this time Mansfield was, presumably, unable to support his growing family without employment of some kind.

Unfortunately for Lord Westbury, his new appointment ended in scandal. He overextended his patronage and allowed his ne'er-do-well son and heir to use his name in discreditable manipulations of his own. Both Lord Westbury's sons were given posts in the Bankruptcy Courts at Exeter. Parkyns' obituary says that he also received a post there, but his name does not appear in the contemporary law list. However both his name and the names of the two Bethells appear in the law list for 1864 under the Bankruptcy Court in London. Unhappily it emerged that the elder of the Bethell sons, apart from specific misdeeds, was himself an undischarged bankrupt. His younger brother was a man of a different stamp who subsequently became a clerk to the House of Lords for thirty years.

The Opposition, supported by a host of those who had suffered under his tongue, seized on the knowledge of Lord Westbury's patronage and other indiscretions with the result that he was obliged to resign his post as Lord Chancellor. He was not regarded as particularly culpable because no one questioned the principle of patronage at the time. However, he had certainly been careless, and Queen Victoria, who had never approved of his choice of words, was indignant at the shadow he had cast over his illustrious office.

Mansfield Parkyns not only survived these upheavals but was soon promoted to be the Comptroller of the Bankruptcy Court, a post which he held, without obvious qualifications, for the next twenty years. What misery and chicanery he must have witnessed! There is no indication of how well he did his work, but there is evidence that he had a talent for detail and was industrious. In the Bankruptcy Courts of the day, recently reformed by Lord Westbury, he had need of both qualities. In addition, one feels sure that he had compassion.

I have only found one letter written by Parkyns during this middle period as a member of the Victorian establishment. In 1876 he was invited to write an article on the Parkyns family by Mr Foster for his new *Peerage and Baronetage*. Writing to a relation at Ruddington for information, Parkyns explained:

> We have been great wanderers . . . but business has oblidged me always to be in reach of Town . . . We tried Worthing and then Petersfield for 3 or 4 years, but sixty miles to work and sixty miles back again for dinner was too much for me: I do not like suburban life for the girls, of which I have eight; and Town still less; so we have gone back to our old home in Nottinghamshire – that is, they are settled there, some of them taking turns to live with me in Town and I go down for long vacations, one of which, I am happy to say, begins next week.

One of his daughters recalled his saying, when they parted after she had done her stint, that he felt as deprived as a monkey losing its fleas because he would have nothing left to pick on.

In London Parkyns had a house in Bayswater Square, well

back from the park, and every day he made the journey to his office in Basinghall Street by the Guildhall in the City. It can have been little to his liking, although, as a result of writing the article in Foster's *Peerage*, he found a new interest in historical genealogy and compiled some impressive work that led to his engaging in a copious correspondence at home and abroad. By now his wife was ill and she died at Woodborough in 1877. In 1884 Mansfield retired to Woodborough and his daughters began to marry, mostly army officers and parsons. We are told by one of his sons-in-law that he lived very quietly and took no part in county affairs. He took a cold bath every day whatever the weather, a reminder perhaps of the spartan life on which he had thrived in his youth.

Locally he was known as 'Abyssinia Parkyns' and had the reputation of being a kindly man. There was hot soup and enough cough mixture at the Hall for anyone who needed it, and he used to visit bedridden invalids to read to them. He had undoubtedly achieved the ambition that had amused Richard Monkton Milnes so many years before, that he should be called 'good Mr Parkyns' behind his back. Indeed it was the only ambition that he had ever voiced. It would have pleased him to know that he was similarly remembered along the route that he had travelled. Samuel Baker, a traveller of a very different sort, wrote in *The Nile Tributaries of Abyssinia*:

> Many years before I visited Wat at Negur (on the Atbara) Mr. Mansfield Parkyns, who has written the best book on Abyssinia that I have ever read, passed through this country. . . . Mr. Parkyns has left behind him what the Arabs call a 'Sweet name'.

Parkyns' main occupation in his last years was the carving, in Gothic style, of new choir stalls and screen for Woodborough Church, in memory of his wife. In this he was assisted by his daughter Sybilla, and by Mr Ward, a local carpenter, who dealt with the heavy joinery. A week after the dedication of his work, Mansfield himself died at the age of 71.

By no stretch of the imagination can Mansfield Parkyns be regarded as an important man. He received no honours in his lifetime and scant mention after his death. He was the exception to Victorian African explorers in that he courted the minimum of attention and was a reluctant author. If the choice

[163]

of biographical subjects were limited to men who participated in important events and left their own record of their achievements, Mansfield Parkyns would not be a candidate; but biography is more truely the study of human nature and the trials to which it is subjected. It is in this context that Mansfield Parkyns so amply deserves consideration. As Galton recognized, it was in his attitude to travel that his true gift lay and in his ability to accord with people of a culture very different to his own without any loss of individuality. Dr Johnson has said that biographies should tell not how a man became great but how he was made happy; and this Mansfield Parkyns' account of his years in Africa most certainly does. The ensuing anticlimax was no less a part of his human lot.

Apart from his book, little remains of Mansfield Parkyns' considerable output of the things that interested him. In his will he divided his estate equally between his daughters, but after a mortgage on Woodborough Hall had been paid off, there was nothing left but his personal possessions, the journal, and the manuscript histories, collected in the Sudan. They provide a rare source of information on certain aspects of the history of that country. Two Arabic texts among his papers in the University of Nottingham are now in the hands of the School of Oriental and African Studies. Also remaining were his paintings, and numerous specimens of African weapons and other artifacts, including a shirt of chainmail from the Kababish tribe. Each had its piece of history for him – lost with his death.

The Wollerton Museum has a good selection of his stuffed birds. In his lifetime these had stood in five glass cases in the entrance hall at Woodborough where he must have passed them many times a day: brilliant reminders – to him alone – of his days in the sun and silence of the Mareb Valley.

Bibliography

Abbadie, Arnauld, d' *Douze ans dans la Haute-Éthiopie* (Paris: 1868).

Abir, Mordechai, *Ethiopia: The Era of the Princes* (London: Longman, 1968).

Blanc, H., *A Narrative of Captivity in Abyssinia* (London: Smith Elder & Co., 1868).

Bruce, James, *Travels to Discover the Source of the Nile in the Years 1768–1773* (5 vols, Edinburgh: J. Ruthxen, 1790).

Burton, R.F., *First Footsteps in East Africa* (London: Longmans & Co., 1856).

Cheesman, R.E., *Lake Tana and the Blue Nile* (London: Frank Cass & Co., 1936).

——'The upper water of the Blue Nile', in *The Geographical Journal*, vol. ixxi, no. 4, pp. 358–76

Combes, E. and Tamister, M., *Voyage en Abyssinie* (4 vols., Paris: 1838).

Combes, E., *Voyage en Egypte et Nubie, etc.* (Paris: 1846).

Crummey, Donald, *Priests and Politicians: Protestant and Catholic Missions in Orthodox Ethiopea, 1830–1868* (Oxford: Clarendon Press, 1972).

Dufton, H. *Narrative of a Journey through Abyssinia in 1862–1863* (London: 1867).

Dwight, H.G., *Constantinople Old and New* (London: Longmans & Co., 1915).

Dye., W.McE., *Moslem Egypt and Christian Abyssinia* (New York: Atkin & Prout, 1880).

Ebers, G., *Egypt, Descriptive, Historical and Picturesque*, trans. Clara Bell (2 vols., London: Cassell & Co., 1881–2).

Eden, F., *The Nile Without a Dragoman* (London: 1871).

Edwards, A.B., *Pharaohs, Fellahs and Explorers* (London: Osgood & McIlvaine, 1891).

——*A Thousand Miles Up the Nile* (London: 1876).

Elgood, Lt . Col.P.G., *The Transit of Egypt* (London: E. Arnold & Co., 1928).

Ferret, P.V.A. and Galinier, J.G., *Voyages en Abyssinie* (Paris: 1847).

Galton, Francis, *The Art of Travel; or Shifts and Contrivances Available in*

Wild Countries, 1st ed., (London: Murray, 1855). Reprinted as *Francis Galton's Art of Travel* with an introduction by Dorothy Middleton (David Charles reprints, 1971).

Gobat, Samuel, *Journal of a Three Years' Residence in Abyssinia* (London: 1834).

Halls, J.J., *The Life and Correspondence of Henry Salt* (2 vols., London: 1934).

Harris, W.C., *The Highlands of Æthiopia* (3 vols., London: 1844).

Hericourt, Rochet d', *Voyage sur la côte orientale de la Mer Rouge dans la pays d'Adel et le royaume Choa*, (Paris: 1841).

——*Second voyage sur les deux rives de la Mer Rouge, etc.* (Paris: 1846).

Hill, Richard, *On the Frontiers of Islam: Two Manuscripts Concerning the Sudan under Turco-Egyptian Rule, 1822–1845* (Oxford: Clarendon Press, 1970).

Holland, T.J. and Hozier, H.M., *Record of the Expedition to Abyssinia* (2 vols., London 1870).

Holt, P.M., *Political and Social Change in Modern Egypt* (London: OUP, 1968).

Hoskins, G.A. *Travels in Ethiopia* (London: Longman, 1835).

Hotton, J.C. *Abyssinia and its People* (1868).

Hyatt, H.M., *The Church of Abyssinia* (London:Luzact & Co. [Oriental Research Series], 1928).

Isaacs, A.A., *The Captive Missionary* (London: 1868).

Isenberg, C.W. and Krapf, J.L., *Journals (1839–1842)* (London: 1843).

James, F.L., *The Wild Tribes of the Sudan* (London: John Murray, 1883).

Johnson, Samuel, [*Rasselas*], *The Prince of Abyssinia* (London: 1759).

Johnston, Charles, *Travels in Southern Abyssinia* (London: 1844).

Kinglake, Alexander, *Eothen (London:* 1844).

Krapf, J.L., *Travels, Researches and Missionary Labours in East Africa* (London: 1860).

Kusel, Baron de *An Englishman's Recollection of Egypt, 1863–1887* (London: John Lane: 1915).

Lane, F.W., *The Manners and Customs of the Modern Egyptians* (London: John Murray, 1860).

Lefebvre, C. Theophile, *Voyage en Abyssinie, executé pendant les années 1839–1843* (6 vols., Paris: 1845–51).

Linant de Bellefonds, *Mémoires sur les principaux travaux d'utillité publique éxecutés en Egypte* (Paris: 1872).

Lipsky, G., *Ethiopea, its People, its Society, its Culture* (New Haven: Hraf Press, 1960).

Lobo, J., *A Voyage to Abyssinia*, translated from the French of le Grande by Samuel Johnson (Hitch, London: A. Bettersworth & C., 1735).

Longrigg, S.H. *A Short History of Eritrea* (Oxford: Clarendon Press 1945).

Markham, C.R., *A History of the Abyssinian Expedition* (London: 1869).

Maydon, H.C., *Simien: Its Heights and Abysses* (London: H.F. & G. Witherby, 1925).

Mayo, Earl of, *Sport in Abyssinia: or the Mareb and Tackazzee* (London: John Murray 1876).

Milnes, Richard, Monckton, *Palm Leaves* (London: E. Moxon 1844).

Pankhurst, Richard, *The Ethiopean Royal Chronicles* (London: 1967).

——*An Introduction to the Economic History of Ethiopea* (London: 1961).

Pallme, I., *Travels in Kordofan* (London: 1844) translated from German.

Parkyns, Mansfield, *Life in Abyssinia* (London: John Murray, 1853).

——'The Kubbabish Arabs, between Dongola and Kordofan', in the Geographical Journal. vol. xx (1851).

Pearce, Nathanial, *Life in Abyssinia,* ed. J.J. Halls (2 vols., London: 1831).

Perham, Marjorie, *The Government of Ethiopia* (London: Faber & Faber, 1969).

Phillips, W.A., 'Mohamet Ali', in *Cambridge Modern History* Vol. X, Ch. 17.

Plowden, Walter, C., *Correspondence respecting Abyssinia 1846–1868,* London: 1868 Parliamentary Papers.

——*Travels in Abyssinia and the Galla Country* (London: 1868).

Poole, S. Lane, *Stratford Canning, Viscount de Redclyffe* (2 vols., London: Longmans, 1888).

Pope-Hennessy, J., *Monckton Milnes: The Flight of Youth* (London: Constable, 1951).

Rassam, H., *Narrative of the British Mission to Theodore King of Abyssinia* (London: 1869).

Reid, J.M., *Traveller Extraordinary: The Life of James Bruce of Kinnaird* (London: Eyre and Spottiswoode, 1968).

Robinson, R., Gallager and Denny, *Africa and the Victorians.* (London: Macmillan, 1961).

Rubenson, Sven, *King of Kings Tewodros of Ethiopia* (Addis Ababa: 1966).

Salt, Henry, *A Voyage to Abyssinia* (London: 1814). Account of Salt's second journey.

Seton-Watson, R.W., *Disraeli, Gladstone and the Eastern Question* (London: Macmillan & Co, 1933).

Starkie, Enid, *Arthur Rimbaud in Abyssinia* (Oxford: Clarendon Press, 1937).

Stern, Revd., H.A., *Wanderings Among the Falashas in Abyssinia* (London: 1862).

——*The Captive Missionary* (London: 1868).

Thakeray, W.M., *Notes of a Journey From Cornhill to Grand Cairo* (London: Chapman & Hall, 1846).

[167]

Trimingham, J.S., *Islam in Ethiopia* (London: OUP, 1952).

Tritton, A.S., *The Caliphs and their Non-Muslim Subjects* (London: OUP, 1930).

Ullendorff, Edward, *The Ethiopians*, 3rd. edn. (London: OUP, 1973).

Urquhart, David, *The Spirit of The East* (2 vols., London: 1844).

Valentia, Viscount, George Annesley, *Voyages and Travels to India, Ceylon, the Red Sea, Abyssinia, and Egypt. 1802–1806* (3 vols., London: William Miller, 1809), containing account of Henry Salt's first expedition.

Waghorn, Thomas, Lieut. R.N., *Egypt as it is in 1837* (London: 1838).

——*Messers Waghorn and Co.'s Overland Guide to India by three routes to Egypt*, 2nd ed. (London: 1844).

——*Particulars of an Overland Journey from London to Bombay, by way of the Continent, Egypt and the Red Sea.* (London: privately printed, 1831).

Wallace, D.M., *Egypt and the Egyptian Question* (London: Macmillan & Co, 1883).

Warburton, Bartholomew Eliot, *The Crescent and the Cross: or the Romance and Reality of Eastern Travel* (2 vols., London: H. Colburn, 1838).

Waterton, Charles, *Wanderings in South America* (London: J. Mawman, 1825).

Werne, Ferdinand, *Expedition to Discover the Sources of the White Nile in the Years, 1840–1841* (2 vols), translated from the German by C.W. O'Reilly (London: 1849).

——*African Wanderings* vol. 10, translated from the German by J.R. Johnston, (London: The Traveller's Library, 1850).

Index